Rethinking learning in early childhood education

Rethinking learning in early childhood education

Nicola Yelland, Libby Lee,
Maureen O'Rourke and Cathie Harrison

 Open University Press

Open University Press
McGraw-Hill Education
McGraw-Hill House
Shoppenhangers Road
Maidenhead
Berkshire
England
SL6 2QL

email: enquiries@openup.co.uk
world wide web: www.openup.co.uk

and Two Penn Plaza, New York, NY 10121-2289, USA

First published 2008

A catalogue record of this book is available from the British Library

ISBN-13: 978-0-335-22882-9 (pb)   978-0-335-22881-2 (hb)
ISBN-10: 0-335-22882-8 (pb)   0-335-22881-X (hb)

Library of Congress Cataloging-in-Publication Data
CIP data applied for

Typeset by RefineCatch Limited, Bungay, Suffolk
Printed in Great Britain by Bell and Bain Ltd., Glasgow

The *McGraw·Hill* Companies

Contents

The important thing is not to stop questioning.
(Albert Einstein)

We dedicate this book to the amazing teachers and children who collaborated in this project and who so willingly shared the exploration of possibilities and complexities with us. It is also for our own children – Caja, Tamsyn, Caleb, Jesse, Ross, Brendan, Sarah and Emma – who give our lives meaning and purpose.

Acknowledgements

There are many people and organizations who have supported us throughout the life of this project. This research would not have been possible without the support of the Australian Research Council (ARC) and our partners, IBM (Asia-Pacific), The Australian National Schools Network, SDN Children's Services (NSW), KU Children's Services (NSW), The Department of Education and Training (NSW), The Department of Education and Training (Western Australia) and the Victorian Schools Innovations Commission. We would like to acknowledge and thank the amazing early childhood educators who shared their professional lives and experiences with us and who let us into their centres and classrooms so frequently. We were generously supported by wonderful research assistants. Anna Kilderry's detailed observations and notes captured the richness of our conversations with teachers and children. In particular, her work in compiling and writing the story of George the Builder was especially important. Sandra Hesterman's PhD was partially funded to conduct research in the project – thank you for sharing your Star Wars scenario with us in Chapter 4. Kylie Montague gave invaluable support to the New South Wales component of the data collection. We thank Rebecca Beris for her amazing effort in compiling the final version of the manuscript. Finally, there are those who keep us going – our family and friends who support us whatever we do and wherever we are. You know who you are, and you make all the difference!

About the authors

Nicola Yelland is Professor of Education in the School of Education at Victoria University in Melbourne, Australia. In the past decade she has conducted research projects which have been concerned with rethinking curriculum and pedagogies with new technologies. This has involved working in varied school contexts with teachers and children to explore the ways in which learning in the twenty-first century can not only lead to improved outcomes but also be relevant to the lives of young people growing up in the information age. She is the author and editor of numerous books including *Critical Issues in Early Childhood* and *Shift to the Future: Rethinking Learning with New Technologies in Education*.

Libby Lee is a Senior Lecturer in Early Childhood Education at Murdoch University in Perth, Western Australia. Her teaching and research interests are focused on early childhood education. Her areas of special interest include the early years curriculum, social justice and the use of technologies to support teaching and learning. Libby's current research focuses on partnerships between Indigenous communities and schools, in particular the transition from home to school, school engagement and retention, and educational outcomes of young Indigenous children.

Maureen O'Rourke is Executive Director of *EdPartnerships International* and has taught in higher education, preschool, primary, secondary and specialist schools. She has worked as an educator in Australia and the USA and provided professional learning programmes for teachers in the Asia-Pacific region. Her research work has been characterized by co-researcher partnerships with teachers, particularly in relation to multiliteracies and use of ICT. More recently, she has focused on an exciting Creative Partnerships programme that has linked teachers and students with a range of industry professionals who have facilitated the development, deep discipline knowledge and rigour in student performances and texts.

Cathie Harrison is a Senior Lecturer in Early Childhood Education at the Australian Catholic University in Sydney. Cathie's research interests include early childhood pedagogy, social justice and giftedness in early childhood. She is the author of the books *Giftedness in Early Childhood* and *Young Gifted Children: Their Search for Complexity and Connection*. Cathie has a diverse range of experience within early childhood education as an academic, teacher, advisor to the ABC television programme *Play School*, and as a consultant to a number of museum and community projects. Her work has been strongly influenced by the early childhood educational experience in Reggio Emilia, Italy and Scandinavia.

1 New millennium learners

> The illiterate of the 21st century will not be those who cannot read and write, but those who cannot learn, unlearn and relearn.
>
> (Alvin Toffler, *Future Shock*)

Introduction

As we move through the first decade of the twenty-first century it has become increasingly apparent that there is a growing disparity between what goes on in schools and in the world outside. New technologies have engendered new work and social practices that have profoundly changed the ways that we do things in our lives, yet schools seem to remain immune to change and maintain a heritage curriculum that was founded in a different age for a different set of circumstances and purposes. The rate of change in society has been tremendous. The children who attend our schools today were born on the cusp of the twenty-first century and, together with those born after 1985, have been called the 'millennial generation' (Howe and Strauss 2000). Their lives are digital and they communicate in a variety of modes with myriad materials that are made of bits and bytes. Their homes are full of media options that include TVs, mobile phone, computers, MP3 players, DVD machines, digital cameras, interactive toys and games, video game consoles and mobile devices. In a comprehensive study of 0–6 year-olds' use of electronic media, Rideout *et al.* (2003) reported that 99% have a TV at home and 36% have one in their own bedroom. Nearly a half of their sample had a video game player and 63% lived in a home that had Internet access. Additionally, nearly half (48%) of under-6s have used a computer and 30% played video games. Parent reports indicate that this group spent approximately 2 hours a day using screen media and that this was about the same as the amount of time that they spent playing outdoors and three times as much time as they spent reading (books) or being read to.

The report continues by suggesting that many of the toddlers and pre-schoolers surveyed are not passively consuming media purchased by their family, but rather are actively seeking out information or helping themselves to acquire it with the various electronic media at their disposal. Seventy-seven% are turning on the TV by themselves, asking for particular shows (67%), using the remote control to change channels (62%), playing their favourite DVDs (71%), turning on the computer by themselves (33%) and loading CD-ROMs with games on (23%). The study revealed that listening to music (and dancing/acting) is one of the most popular pastimes for young children in this age range with 79% listening to music daily and just under half (42%) owning their own CD player so they can listen when they want to.

Children in the next age range (6–17 years) continue to diversify their practices with new media. Over 2 million American children in this cohort have created their own website and there are similar trends in the UK (Gibson 2005; Livingstone and Bober n.d.). More recently the evolution of social media such as MySpace, Facebook and Captain Penguin and the growing use of blogs, wikis and instant messaging enable young people to be in touch almost constantly with all their friends and families. These new lifeworlds require us to reconceptualize forms of communication and notions of identity that are so essential for effective learning in schools. These technologies play different roles in the lives of children for different purposes at different junctures in time and in a variety of communities of practice (Lave and Wenger 1990).

In this book we will use the terms 'new technologies' and 'information and communications technologies' (ICT) interchangeably to include the groups of things that incorporate computers, digital cameras and televisions, MP3 players, mobile telephony, electronic whiteboards, scanners, electronic musical instruments, laser printers, as well as the software that is associated and runs with the various pieces of hardware, such as the Internet, communications software like Skype and Messenger, social media (e.g. MySpace, Facebook), editing programs such as iMovie and Moviemaker, Garage Band, Kid Pix, and the suite of Microsoft programs that includes PowerPoint, Word and Excel. All these artefacts are regarded as resources which children can use depending on the context that they find themselves in and the purpose of what they are doing. Conversely, 'old technologies' include pencils, crayons and pens, blackboards, textbooks and overhead projectors.

Learning twenty-first century skills

In thinking about recent trends and policies in education it becomes apparent that there has been a global focus on student achievement in terms of a narrowly focused set of demonstrable criteria based in what are perceived as being the 'basics' of literacy and numeracy. This has been contextualized in an environment of cautious conservatism and justified on the grounds that teachers should be accountable to the public for the welfare of the children in their care and that there are indeed a set of finite and measurable items that are generally regarding as being the core or foundation for later understandings. Such views have been enacted in policies such as 'No Child Left Behind' (United States Department of Education 2001) and reflected in the popular media with newspapers and current affairs programmes deploring the lack of 'heritage basic skills' of students in our schools today, based on testing regimes that existed some 50 years ago or more. Many would argue that these fundamental skills and knowledge underpin everything that we do despite the prevalence of new technologies, and perhaps they are a starting point. However, their influence permeates all aspects of the heritage curriculum, and teachers often complain that preparation for the tests ensures that they have little time for other activities beyond the basics.

A report by the Partnership for 21st Century Skills (n.d.) recognizes that we need to define and incorporate core subjects in order to establish the conditions to extend thinking from a foundational base, but recommends that we extend our notion of what is 'basic' in light of the significant changes that have occurred in all aspects of our lives over the past decade and longer. They note that No Child Left Behind identifies the core subjects as being English, reading or language arts, mathematics, science, foreign languages, civics, government, economics, arts, history and geography, and applaud the fact that the list was expanded to meet the demands of the new century. However, they also contend that citizens of the twenty-first century need to go beyond the core subjects in order to function effectively and that they need to know how to use their knowledge and skills to:

- think critically
- apply knowledge to new contexts
- analyse information
- understand new ideas
- communicate
- solve problems
- make decisions.

The committee members regard such skills as being learning skills that are increasingly important in the workplace and for community lives to be enriched. Further, they outline three areas of learning skills that are based around:

- information and communication
- thinking and problem solving
- interpersonal and self-directional skills.

They stated that 'Learning skills enable people to acquire new knowledge and skills, connect new information to existing knowledge, analyse, develop habits of learning and work with others to use information among other skills' (p. 10). This then energizes learners to be autonomous and flexible in their learning so that they can adapt well to the changing circumstances that tend to define our contemporary lives. Naturally, the resources that support the learning skills are digital and facilitate interactions and learning that were not possible prior to their development.

The committee also propose a strategy to assist children to make connections in their learning to build on this. Teachers should be cognizant of them as they include:

- making content relevant to children's lives
- bringing the world into the classroom
- taking students out into the world
- creating contexts for learning that enable students to interact with themselves and others in authentic ways.

A perspective such as this resonates with what Scardamalia (2003) calls 'knowledge building', which she maintains should be central to the process of education. Scardamalia defines knowledge building as:

> the production and continual improvement of ideas of value to a community, through means that increase the likelihood that what the community accomplishes will be greater than the sum of individual contributions and part of broader cultural efforts . . . as applied to education . . . the approach means engaging learners in the full process of knowledge creation.
>
> (p. 2)

Scardamalia contends that a focus on knowledge building will enable schools to become effective sites to foster creativity and innovation. Such skills are fundamental for effective functioning in the twenty-first century. In this book we take the view that children bring a wide range of knowledge, skills and dispositions to school from their homes and communities and that this should be valued and extended. Schools then can become places where public knowledge is explored, experimented with and modified in active and specific ways with the purpose of using it in new and creative ways. New millennium learners make sense and extend their knowledge using new technologies and communicate their findings both locally and globally.

Education in a contemporary world

It is often claimed that the purpose of education is to prepare people for productive lives in society. In traditional Western education systems, the goal was related to generating workers for the various levels of work in industrial capitalism. This meant that, at the production level, jobs were routine in nature, repetitive in sequence and there was no room for querying the protocols of the operation. At the other end of the spectrum, higher-order skills were needed by a managerial class to set them apart from those whom they organized. In contemporary times the world of business, commerce and industry has changed as a result of the tremendous range of scientific and technological innovations. This has meant that a new range of employment opportunities have opened up that are very different from the old system. Routine and mechanical production lines have been transposed to developing countries where they can be completed for a fraction of the cost in the West. New opportunities have arisen for creative, innovative and collaborative workers who can generate ideas for new products and services. These people can deal with abstract ideas and are able to adapt to changing times fluently. A wide range of workers seem to have been exposed to the consumerism that characterizes capitalism, and this in turn generates new ideas and products that can be sold to devour increased amounts of disposable income from a growing proportion of the world population.

However, there are still those who are increasingly being characterized as contract, temporary, manual, itinerant or migrant workers and who rarely share the benefits of the new capitalism, despite being the major contributors to its success.

It is becoming increasingly evident that schools have changed minimally from those that propped up the old capitalism, even though global societies and economies require that they produce workers for the new capitalism. Here is where a contradiction exists. Governments in the West maintain that they need to lead the world in terms of innovation and design of new products to supply the consumer market, yet they are obsessed with promoting heritage schooling systems that have as their focus the rote learning of skills and memorization of content for tests of knowledge acquisition as major indicators of success for the system.

In this book we argue that in order for our children to live meaningful lives in the twenty-first century we need to have an education system that stimulates students to acquire and practise (new) skills so that they are able to build new knowledge beyond that which we already have. We believe that this can be achieved via authentic and engaging activities, by collaborating with others, by seeking out expert assistance and knowledge from a variety of sources and by sharing the findings with a wide audience. Interestingly, business leaders and other employers have articulated the same goals about what is needed for an effective contemporary workforce. Yet at the same time they deplore and criticize young people for not being able to demonstrate skills that were heralded in past times with old technologies. It is apparent that being able to generate, think, inquire, collaborate, critique and communicate ideas and knowledge is relevant to all disciplines or domains of knowledge. These can be regarded as the *new basics* of the twenty-first century. Yet our education systems are still structured around privileged content that has existed for generations despite the fact that evidence from numerous research projects suggests that new technologies are able to transform learning. (e.g. (Tinker 1999; Yelland 1997).

The majority of educational theories relating to learning (e.g. Bruner 1977; Piaget 1972; Vygotsky 1978) that underpin Western education systems are grounded in the belief that humans learn best when they are engaged and actively constructing meaning. This enables learners to explore and solve problems in environments where they are able to take risks and learn from their mistakes. Nearly 30 years ago, Papert (1980) provided a vision for educators that encouraged the use of computers as objects that could extend thinking and the generation of new ideas. This was groundbreaking since it meant that technology had the potential to extend children's experiences in ways that were not previously possible. Notions of abstract and concrete had to be reconceptualized as the new machines enabled young learners to visualize and manipulate materials and gain new insights and understandings about how they functioned and related to each other.

However, as Cuban (1993) has observed, this vision has not yet materialized and many schools remain much the same, in terms of the content of curriculum and the types or methods of teaching that are used, despite advances in the use of new technologies. Accordingly, while there is a recognition that these are *new times* (Hall and Jacques, 1989), many schools are locked into an existence that seems to be better characterized as old times, with curricula that were conceived in the industrial rather than the information age.

New learning

Kalantzis and Cope (2008) have suggested that we need a broader view of learning than currently exists and thus conceptualized *new learning* in order to consider what people need to *know* and *do* in contemporary society. They posit that this is, in fact, very different from what currently exists in formal schooling and thus contrast this new learning to the old learning grounded in heritage curricula which prepared citizens for a very different era and set of societal, political and economic circumstances. This includes eight dimensions for new learning that they regard as critical:

1   *The social significance of education:* located at the centre of the knowledge economy, acting as a mechanism for social justice and equitable outcomes.

2   *The institutional locations of learning:* are broadened to include multiple sites (including schools) and their function goes beyond learning bodies of knowledge in traditional disciplines to include learning how to learn in diverse modes and ways.

3   *The tools for learning:* that include new technologies which have transformed our lives and enabled learning in new ways that need to be accommodated in educational contexts.

4   *The outcomes of learning:* shift from being individualized and cognitive to add the dimensions of sensibility, capability and collaborative learning so that building new knowledge is possible.

5   *The balance of agency:* is shared between participants in learning environments so that learners are able not only to use existing knowledge but also to transform it to new knowledge that has some relevance and application for societies.

6   *The significance of difference:* where those who do not 'fit' the educational model are not discarded but valued and included as participants, thus creating educational contexts that are characterized by justice, fairness and equity.

7   *The relations of the old to the new:* whereby the old is transformed into new learning so that it has contemporary relevance.

8   *The professional role of the teacher:* changes from purveyor of knowledge to being an autonomous, responsible designer of student learning who is a valued member of the community, a partner in learning, a researcher and social scientist.

Kalantzis and Cope (2008) do not recommend a new learning system or curriculum, but rather suggest that it is a series of open possibilities in response to specific questions that are raised by teachers in myriad circumstances. They suggest that posing questions such as 'What might we do?' places the teacher in an engaged, intellectual and professional sphere that varies from what they previously experienced. Teachers have mandated curriculum and some have syllabus documents that guide what they do with the students in their class. New learning engages them in interrogations about curriculum, pedagogies and the design of learning activities than enable them to be implemented in more relevant and dynamic ways that incorporate the effective use of ICT to deepen understandings and transform the communication of ideas and knowledge.

New learning recognizes that workers in the new millennium and beyond 'require skills and sensibilities that are significantly different from those of the past' (Australian Council of Deans of Education 2001: 31). The argument for new learning is based on the fact that education should be sensitive to the needs of new times. For example, new technologies have reshaped the relationship between knowledge and the technological tools that we use. We need to be collaborative, multi-skilled and flexible so that we are able to extend our range of activities in order to solve problems and create new conditions for transformation. New economies and workplaces are places of diversity, and cultures of work are established and continually evolving. Such activities are knowledge based and do not rely on rote mechanistic actions. This is a major change and those who are able to make the transition are the most effective knowledge workers of the twenty-first century.

Thus, new learning enables us to consider the ways in which we might reconceptualize and organize knowledge for new times and identifies the characteristics of the new citizen and the skills base required for them to function effectively in twenty-first-century society. Accordingly, new learning environments (Kalantzis *et al.* 2005: 7):

- support a culture of innovation where risk taking is encouraged
- provide contexts for collaborative learning
- encourage problem posing and strategic thinking
- establish learners as autonomous and outward looking
- promote higher-order thinking that draws from various knowledge bases and perspectives
- cultivate a capacity for lifelong and lifewide learning
- encourage sharing and communication of ideas using multimodal methods and the use of new technologies.

Diversity

Contemporary times are characterized by apparently continuous cycles of changes and growth in new technologies that influence how we do everyday things and communicate with others. We live in a time in which we can connect with a range of people across the world via new media, and this has changed the dynamics of whom we meet and interact with in different ways. Our lifeworlds incorporate the local and the global, the real and the virtual, and the boundaries between them seem to be fading and becoming increasingly irrelevant. Such diverse communities are created and sustained for a multitude of reasons and their impact is significant since they enable us to relate to each other as citizens, workers, friends and consumers. In fact, diversity is one of the most pervasive features of these new times, and thus postmodern perspectives characterized by heterogeneity, multiple discourses and recognitions about the complexity of diversity and emancipated by critiques of universal truths and structures are useful to help us to understand the nature of the individuals and groups that exist (Harvey 1989). In extending this notion, it is becoming apparent that unless schools address the notion of diversity and consider how students might engage with ideas and experiences, they are in danger of becoming obsolete. As educators, we need to figure out how to make education relevant for a diverse population so that it is possible for each person to engage and, as a consequence, learn. As noted by Kalantzis *et al.* (2005: 46–7):

> Learning succeeds or fails to the extent that it engages the varied subjectivities of learners. Engagement produces opportunity, equity and participation. Failure to engage produces failure, disadvantage and inequality . . . engagement must be with learners in their lifeworld reality, and that reality is marked by extraordinary difference.

Rethinking learning

Thus, the starting point for rethinking learning is to find ways to engage with the diverse lifeworlds that young children bring to early educational contexts. The project that forms the basis of this book sought to address some of the issues related to this by creating a research partnership with early childhood educators to reconceptualize their pedagogies so that they afforded opportunities for children from diverse backgrounds to use their experiences and knowledge base as a springboard for learning. We realized that children come to school with a rich repertoire of knowledge and experiences. In order to build on them we needed to know what they were and how to extend them in meaningful and appropriate ways. This resonated with the work of Moll *et al.* (1992) who recognized community 'funds of knowledge' which supported early learning. Additionally, it required educators to go beyond thinking about formal learning as sets of skills and knowledge that needed to be reproduced or demonstrated in set pieces. There was a recognition that contemporary times were characterized by new ways of working that incorporated the use of ICT and a concomitant view that a new view of literacy – characterized as multiliteracies (New London Group 1996) located in multimodal representations and forms of communication – was needed.

Thus, in Chapter 2, we describe the context of the project and the ways in which we collaborated with teachers in order to achieve our goals for rethinking learning. Making education relevant to the lives of young children and their families was at the core of this research, and we knew that we could not achieve this with traditional research methods. Our research design was created with the teachers, and we co-constructed the direction and form that unfolded. We started with broad goals and aims and some idea of how we thought these might be achieved, but we were flexible in how they might be reached. We introduced the pedagogy of multiliteracies to our first group of preschool teachers and followed up on what it might look like in preschool settings across a range of contexts. This is described in Chapter 3, so that readers are able to have a clear view of where we were starting and what a multiliteracies perspective might look like in early childhood education. We illustrate the main points from existing literature and with examples from our research data throughout this book. Our aim is to share new ways of working with young children that embrace their lifeworlds and show how teachers can support diverse learners by building on their strengths. Teachers have milestones for achievement that they themselves formulate, and others that are dictated by mandated curricula. We worked with teachers to design ways of achieving these via alternative pathways so that each learner was provided with opportunities to extend their existing knowledge and skills and also encouraged to move beyond print literacy as the primary medium of communication and representation. We believe that contemporary times are characterized by multimodal literacies that need to be used and under-stood as alternative forms of communication, and a discussion of what this means forms the basis of Chapter 4. There we provide examples from two individual cases as well as from an early years innovation project and a themed project based on a group of students' fascination with the *Star Wars* phenomenon.

In Chapters 5 and 6, we discuss issues of identity and diversity and how they impact on learning opportunities for young children. The issues are illustrated via the use of cases of young children who were focus children in the project and studied for 3 years. We documented their learning from preschool into the first years of school and draw out some salient points in relation to ways in which we might promote and support identity formation and work with diversity in the early years.

Our multiliteracies portrait, pedagogies and pathways framework is described and illustrated by using a sample from one of our focus children in Chapter 7. It was designed, modified and used by the teachers over a period of 18 months in the second half of the project. In working with the teachers it became evident that our work with multiliteracies and ICT needed to be documented so that teachers could plan effectively for future learning. The multiliteracies framework was used by the teachers with those children who were experiencing difficulties with learning so that they could seek alternative pathways to support them for the future. It enabled them to come to understand the learner more clearly by identifying their strengths as a starting point. Further, it prompted them to think of ways in which the child might work in different modes to understand concepts and express ideas. In this way it provided a synthesis of the child from diverse perspectives and considering a range of features compiled by the teachers, the children and their families.

In the final chapter, we summarize our main findings and suggest new pathways for teachers who are ready to take on the exciting challenges of the twenty-first century in our early childhood centres and schools.

2 Collective inquiry and a partnerships approach to change in education

Introduction

In this chapter, we outline the project that informs the content of the book and describe the strategies that we used in it to collaborate with teachers in our work around shared understandings about rethinking learning in early childhood.

The project began in the new millennium at a time when the use of new technologies was increasing rapidly in early childhood centres and schools. At the same time the use of ICT in homes was also prevalent and many parents had purchased computers and other devices on the assumption that their children would be 'left behind' if they did not have access to them and skill in using them. One of the key challenges faced by the education sector is the need to provide teachers with the skills necessary to incorporate ICT effectively into their pedagogical repertoire (Becker 2000; Piannfetti 2001). Research has shown that we cannot naturally assume that teachers have the skills base or knowledge of how to use ICT effectively in their design of learning experiences (Elkind 1996; Wartella and Jennings 2000). The foundations for literacy and numeracy are established in the early years, yet we still have little empirical data that documents not only the ways in which new millennium learners comprehend and use digital texts and visual information, but also how they are able to create their own using a variety of media. Until recently, computers have been a peripheral feature of early childhood settings and programmes, but increasingly, since many young children and their families are using them for so many everyday activities, their role has become more essential and relevant.

The project that we embarked upon sought to address some of the issues around the use of ICT in the early childhood years. The broad aim was to consider effective pedagogies for the use of ICT in early childhood centres and classrooms in three Australian states. We designed a collaborative action research project that was undertaken with a network of 36 teachers across the three states. In consultation with the teachers we devised a programme that had as its main goal to establish how ICT can most effectively be used for enhancing children's learning and to identify a range of specific ways in which teachers could build on their existing skills by incorporating ICT (Comber and Green 1999; Green *et al.* 1998). We wanted to empower teachers so they could employ independent, critical thinking in the use of ICT in their teaching environment and thus extend their pedagogical repertoire and create challenging, stimulating and engaging learning opportunities for their children.

Research to date reveals that there is still a vast amount to discover about the learning outcomes for children and for early childhood pedagogy in relation to the use of ICT in early years settings. Some research indicates that computers, in particular, have the potential to be powerful and dynamic influences on learning (e.g. Clements 1999; Papert 1998; Yelland 2002, 2007). However, critics (e.g. Armstrong and Casement 2001; Cordes and Miller 2000; Healy 1998) continue to maintain the stance that young children should not use and play with computers and games machines or be exposed to the dangers of the Internet. Such views contrast developmentalism with the use of new technologies with the protagonists asserting that using new technologies takes away time that can more valuably be spent playing with materials and exposes children to unnecessary danger involving unsuitable material and predators on the Internet (Cordes and Miller 2000).

Educational researchers have created new frameworks for conceptualizing and evaluating the kinds of skills that may be acquired via the use of new technologies in the context of the fast pace of change that is evident in our lives (Monteith 2004). Traditionally, early childhood education was organized around developmentally appropriate practice (DAP) (Bredecamp and Copple 1997) and child-centred curricula (Lee 2002) which posed significant limitations for understanding ICT use. New approaches, such as cross-cultural and postmodern views, have challenged the traditional discourses and provided perspectives on learning and children that are diverse and wide-ranging.

As previously stated, early childhood is the time when the foundations for literacy and numeracy are laid down (Clay 1993), and the need for further research connecting such foundations to the use of ICT in early childhood learning has been clearly established (Department of Education, Science and Training 2002; O'Rourke 2003; Yelland 2001). Our research responded to this by focusing on the broader issue of how a multiliteracies perspective of pedagogy and practice could better guide the role of ICT in facilitating children's learning and, in particular, rethinking literacy and learning.

To achieve this, we undertook a form of collaborative practitioner research where teachers, academic researchers and teacher educators worked in association with a network of 36 teachers in three states in Australia. The specific aims of our research were:

- to establish a pedagogy for multiliteracies in early childhood that would prepare children for today's technology-rich society (including identifying cases of preferred practice for integrating ICT into early childhood environments to facilitate the pedagogy of multiliteracies);
- to design, in collaboration with teachers, approaches to integrating technology into the pre-compulsory and early years school settings that were responsive to current early childhood philosophies;
- to investigate the value of multimedia in relation to the learning needs of minority and disadvantaged groups, including Indigenous children, children from language backgrounds other than English and children with special needs;
- to enable educators to identify the extent of the impact of early access to ICT on children in families from low socio-economic areas;
- to create communities of practice with technology, including mentoring and collegial support groups for professional development, use of online resources and communication tools, and the development of an online network;
- to document and showcase exemplary practice with ICT in early childhood contexts as a means of informing early childhood educators about effective ways to incorporate ICT into programs for optimal learning.

Scope of the project

This project initially involved 12 preschool and childcare centres located in disadvantaged communities in three different states in Australia. This included children with Indigenous backgrounds, recent arrivals with first languages other than English and children with special needs. Each preschool or childcare centre teacher chose two or three children as case studies during the first year of the research. As these children moved on to primary school, their new schools and teachers were invited to join the research project. This invitation extended to teachers of the children for their first two years of primary school. Four university-based researchers (coordinating researchers) worked with the teacher researchers over the 3-year duration of the project and facilitated research circle meetings that occurred four times a year.

The initial selection of teachers was based on prior participation in the *IBM KidSmart Early Learning Program* (IBM Corporation 2000). As such the children involved in the programme already met the following criteria: high incidence of socio-economic disadvantage; high proportion of children and families with language backgrounds other than English; strong links with Indigenous communities; and limited computer access and availability within the local community. As part of the KidSmart program, each centre had been provided with a Young Explorer computer and software. Teachers had engaged in a 12-month professional learning programme that provided training in technical skills, professional reading and discussion to encourage a critical perspective of computer use in early childhood and engagement in a short action research project. The research team led this professional learning programme and conducted statewide evaluations. The evaluation data indicated specific areas as requiring immediate systematic research. These included:

- clarification of effective pedagogy in relation to teaching and learning with ICT in early childhood settings
- investigation of how technological literacy or the foundations of multiliteracies can best be facilitated in early childhood settings
- understanding the impact of multimedia software on children whose first language was other than English
- assessment of the impact of multimedia software on children with disabilities
- clear articulation of the opportunities that ICT presents for new ways of learning
- development of teachers' and parents' understandings in relation to ICT use with young children
- exploration of the impact of early access to ICT on children's first years at school
- examination of the impact of developing use of ICT in preschool settings through peer tutoring.

Consequently, our project was designed to address what constituted effective pedagogy in relation to the use of technology in early childhood when this was associated with the pedagogy of multiliteracies. We also built upon the promising emerging findings that indicated that technology and a multiliterate approach could better enable children's diverse learning pathways, recognizing their diversity and individual learning needs. Our expansion into a broader research project also enabled more systematic tracking and analysis of evidence of impact. What remained constant in our new research was a commitment to working with teachers as learning partners.

Research design and rationale

Two major issues that guided our research design were the consideration of how teachers would directly benefit from engaging in the research and how the design could emphasize research *with* teachers, not *on* them. Thus, we attempted to avoid the traditional stereotype of being researchers who come into educational settings, gather as much data and information as possible, then leave and analyse the data back in a university. The research process was also designed to act as a catalyst for change, a process that supported rethinking and new actions for all involved.

Hopkins (1987) argued that traditional educational research has been inadequate in terms of helping classroom teachers to improve their practice and suggested that one way to make it relevant was to involve the teacher as researcher who was an integral and essential part of the process. This was supported by Stake (1987) who observed that the results of educational research were often framed as either specific or general recommendations and contained few signposts for action. Hopkins (1987: 114) stated that, as a consequence of this, 'teachers often regard educational research as something irrelevant to their lives and see little interaction between the world of the educational researcher and the world of the teacher'. This would appear to apply to Australian teachers who rated participation in academic research projects towards the bottom of a list of preferred methods to gain or improve teaching or administrative skills (Conners 1991).

In planning our project we were clear that we wanted to work collaboratively with teachers to transform practice, and thus create more effective contexts for learning for young children. We realized this would not be possible in the context of traditional research paradigms. Thus, all participants in the research were regarded as researchers, each of whom had different roles and responsibilities, and as members of a collective. Decisions about direction and focus were made as a group, and documentation, planning and analysis of the research artefacts were carried out by each member of the group. Kruger *et al.* (2001) point out that one impact of postmodern research has been to separate researchers in universities and practitioners in schools, both discursively and practically. Their study developed a methodology around the notion of 'collaborative practitioner research' where teachers and university researchers came to a 'co-learning agreement' (Wagner 1997). Wagner (1997: 17) characterized this relationship as being 'reflexive, systematic inquiry, stimulated in part by ongoing collegial communication between researchers and practitioners'. Our methodology was therefore designed around a core strand of collaborative action research which was developed with participatory principles and critical theory in mind. A complementary strand of social inquiry was also developed with an aim to be both reflexive and respectful. This strand of the research drew upon interpretivism, constructivism and critical theory.

The constructivist position meant respecting the worldviews and experiences that all participants brought to the study. By sharing multiple perspectives, we attempted to come to more informed, insightful and sophisticated views. The seeking of multiple perspectives was also considered as a strategy to assist in constructing a view of cultural changes that occurred in teachers' workplaces and classrooms. The constructivist or interpretivist tradition of social inquiry recognizes that the very presence of a researcher is likely to impact on and cause changes in the context; however, this is not the primary goal. Rather it focuses on uncovering new understandings that assist us to explain 'what is' and in turn how this might lead to a rethinking about practices that might be modified or extended as a result of the reflection.

Kincheloe and McLaren (1994) state that critical research is best understood in the context of empowering individuals and as an attempt to confront injustice. They describe this kind of research as 'political' and a transformative endeavour that aims to promote emancipatory consciousness. Critical researchers are clear and unequivocal about their 'partisanship in the struggle for a better world' (1994: 140). Although they enter into the research situation with their assumptions on the table, Kincheloe and McLaren state that these assumptions may change as they are analysed, particularly if the researcher recognizes that such assumptions are not leading to emancipatory actions.

A critical view was particularly important in our research context as all of our research settings were located in areas of low socio-economic status. Children identified by teachers as 'focus children' were diverse in nature, and each teacher selected at least one child who presented as likely to experience challenges in the traditional school setting. By providing access to technology and developing pedagogies that viewed literacy from a multiliteracies perspective, our research programme aimed to encourage such emancipatory actions.

In building on the notion of participatory research, Freire's concept of education – dialogical education – is premised on the following:

> The teacher is no longer merely the one who teaches, for the teacher is also taught in dialogue with the students. And the students, while being taught, also teach. In this way, teacher and students become jointly responsible for a process in which all of them grow.
>
> (Freire 1972: 53)

Freire's views led to calls for research and teaching to be combined (e.g. Kincheloe 1991; Stenhouse 1976) in order to transcend pedagogical routines (Fals Borda 2001). The notion of 'capacitation' emerged from the Brazilian education system as a way of working with teachers that opens spaces for reflection, dialogue, and reinvention of actions, leading to better educational practices (Weber 1992). This is similar to Kemmis's (2001: 100) conceptualization of action research as a process that *'brings people together around shared topical concerns, problems and issues . . .* in a way that will permit people to achieve mutual understanding and consensus about what to do' (emphasis in original). The knowledge creation process in this sense is firmly grounded in experience with theorizing connected to sense making and action planning within the group, rather than being imposed arbitrarily in a disconnected manner from outside. As a result of this, increasing people's self-reliance and empowerment are cited as genuine achievements of participatory research (Fals Borda 2001; Heron and Reason 2001; Kemmis 2001).

Kemmis (2001) suggested a view whereby practitioners should be regarded 'as people who are able to do their own theorizing for themselves, without the intervention of the social scientist as the mediator of what is to count as social reality' (2001: 3). The role of the external researcher needed to shift to one where they could 'engage in, or facilitate, or cooperate with, or collaborate with, or at least support practitioners researching their own practice' (2001: 4).

Maguire (2001: 65) noted a number of feminist influences at the heart of action research which also address power relations: the effort to flatten power by promoting the approach of co-researchers; the notion of 'reflexivity', where researchers critique and change their own research practices in response to identifying power differentials; attempts to make visible and rework the conditions of knowledge production; and clear location of researchers and their biases, feelings, choices and multiple identities within the research process. Gaventa and Cornwall (2001) looked at power and knowledge in the participatory relationship and proposed a different form of knowledge that can emerge through participatory action research. Citing Selener (1997), they noted the following:

- Those who are directly affected by the research problem at hand must participate in the research process, thus democratizing or recovering the power of experts.
- Knowledge is socially constructed and embedded, and therefore research approaches that 'allow for social, group, or collective analysis of life experiences of power and knowledge are most appropriate.
- Participatory action research recognizes different forms of knowing . . . and that feeling and action are as important as cognition and rationality in the knowledge creation process.

When practitioners are precluded from researcher roles, valuable knowledge creation and teacher theorizing are lost, along with the potential for increasing practitioners' capacity for creativity and productive change.

Project methodology

Our methodology was thus based on collaborative practitioner research (Noffke and Stevenson 1995), action research and critical inquiry involving teachers as co-researchers. We built on earlier work by Cherednichenko *et al.* (2001) and addressed recommendations to include both collaborative analysis and theorizing in collaborative practitioner research. Variations of this methodology had been successfully used to identify learning outcomes, confirm understandings about teaching and learning, and enable teachers as researchers to 'identify and speculate on new findings with regard to links between teaching practice, school organisation and student learning' (Cherednichenko *et al.* 2001: 2). Our intention was that our collective research process would also act as a form of professional learning and be of direct benefit to the teachers and their education communities.

The collaborative practitioner research process challenged the traditional divide between teacher practitioners and academic researchers. We sought to connect the reflective insights of teachers in different schools to emerging research propositions. This required us to go beyond action research if we were to reach a stage of proposing generalizable research findings while still being mindful of our study's democratic intentions (Cherednichenko *et al.* 2001). The resolution of this problem was the collaborative analysis and theorizing strategy in reflective action circle (RAC) meetings (O'Rourke 2003) which complemented the reflection and systematic inquiry and documentation by teachers. What resulted was a pathway towards the proposition of *research findings*, which could be accorded the status of fuzzy generalizations (Bassey 2001). The coordinating researchers synthesized a map of connections that emerged from the teacher data, which was then returned to the teacher researchers for further debate and validation. Connections with the literature were also incorporated at this stage. This constituted the collaborative analysis phase. Bassey (2001: 17) also noted that teachers generally seek 'practical guidance based on credible evidence' as opposed to the sociologist who seeks 'theoretical insight based on methodological probity'.

Local insights informed local practice in the spirit of action research. The research also exposed local practice and understanding to a broader evaluation through a final symposium which brought together teachers from all participating schools, the coordinating research team, other interested researchers and education professionals. A further collaborative validation took place following reports by teachers of their local insights, and these were also integrated into our emerging framework of findings. Through the collaborative validations, academic researchers and school colleagues confirmed local interpretations, leading to a mapping of similarities and differences in the form of a multiliteracies portrait, profile and pathways. These validated findings were then available for local testing.

Our research was designed to include practitioners in a process of collaborative theorizing, an inquiry similar to the collaborative analysis stage. Two criteria are necessary for collaborative theorizing. The first is that findings be evaluated as *trustworthy* (Mishler 1990; Yeatman and Sachs 1995) by their explicit connections with practice and the interests of practitioners and their students. Collaborative theorizing must also have the potential for research *validity*, by connecting with research literature and by being available for public scrutiny, using, for example, the public tests of validity outlined by Anderson and Heer (1999). They proposed five validity tests: outcome (research leads to resolution of problem); process (research allows for learning); democratic (research is collaborative); catalytic (research leads to understanding and transformation); and dialogic (research accorded peer review).

During our final research circle meetings, teachers identified examples of children's social practice that aligned with the revised multiliteracies pedagogical framework. The act of translating theory into practice and practice into theory led to significant insights being reported by both teacher and coordinating researchers. Collaborative theory building was not only desirable but also a crucial aspect of the knowledge creation process.

We recognize that as coordinators, researchers were in a position to shape the experiences of the teachers (and therefore in a position of power). We had a clear, yet flexible, agenda for the project in terms of enacting the pedagogy of multiliteracies via the incorporation of ICT and an increased awareness about what children bring to learning contexts from their families and communities. Our approach can be characterized as a catalyst for action in this respect. We provided literature and conversations, prompted reflections and discussions and suggested strategies that might be relevant and appropriate to try in the various settings. The teachers remained enthusiastic about the ideas being shared and very frequently adapted them to suit their local conditions, especially in the latter part of the project when the portrait, pedagogies and pathways documentation was being created.

More recent work on praxis inquiry also supports our approach. Gudjónsdóttir *et al.* (2007) developed four iterative dimensions to build habits of reflective practice and to engage in practice-theory writing in action, which we have adapted to align with our teacher researchers (Table 2.1). The four iterations can be mapped across our research as our teachers maintained learning stories and sets of artefacts of children's work, met regularly in reflect-

Table 2.1 Praxis inquiry

PRACTICE DESCRIBED	PRACTICE EXPLAINED
Teacher researchers describe practice (cases, artefacts, anecdotes) and identify questions (what do I wonder about when I think about this event?)	Teacher researchers seek to discover professional explanations for their practice (literature, research, mentors and colleagues, teacher education – how can I understand this practice?)
PRACTICE THEORIZED	**PRACTICE CHANGED**
Teacher researchers consider the overriding question: who am I becoming as an educator as I integrate these understandings and beliefs into my practice? (who am I becoming as a teacher?)	Teacher researchers plan action (how can I act to improve learning for students and improve my capacity as an educator? what are my new questions?)

ive action circles to present and interpret their observations and examined children's work. Ultimately these actions led to them rethinking their practice and developing a greater sense of professionalism and confidence. As time went on, teachers became increasingly confident about contributing to the emerging multiliteracies theoretical framework and played a vital role in the construction of our portrait, pedagogy and pathways findings.

Reflective action circles and learning partnerships

Our methodology incorporated the use of reflective action circles (O'Rourke 2003) which were held three or four times per year and took the form of cluster meetings at early childhood centres or schools, facilitated by the coordinating researchers in each state. The RACs enabled educators to be active researchers in their own teaching situation and to share their ideas and experiences in a professional forum. They were also a strategy for encouraging further building of professional skills through ongoing action research in the early education settings. Early childhood professionals were also provided with access to current research and expertise in ICT and assisted to develop site-based action research and learning stories of their focus children. The RACs expanded each year to invite new teachers of the focus children.

Mentoring partnerships

We took the view that mentoring partnerships are central to professional exchange and the extension of expertise in early education settings. Research has indicated that early childhood professionals have a strong preference for working with each other (e.g. Fleer 2001). This is because they gain the most influential insights from interactions with others working in similar situations and experiencing similar challenges. The RACs provided the opportunities for preschool teachers to become mentor teachers in relation to their primary school colleagues who initially had not had exposure to the concept of multiliteracies and the ways of using ICT that were consistent with the pedagogy of multiliteracies.

Early professional learning activities provided time for teachers to reflect upon themselves, their views of literacy and issues they felt passionate about in relation to children's learning. Time was also provided for teachers to expand their technical knowledge in relation to the use of ICT for educational purposes.

Each coordinating researcher facilitated group meetings and workshops with the teacher researchers in their state, approximately four times per year, and visited the classrooms of the focus children at least three times per year. Collaborative analysis took place during the RAC meetings with teachers and additional meetings of the coordinating researchers, who prepared summary findings to discuss and interrogate with teachers.

All teachers in the project group planned an action research project and engaged in tracking the learning and literacy practices of their focus children, with a given emphasis on how children engaged with and made use of ICT in the classroom. Teachers met each term to discuss progress in relation to the inquiries and to engage in discussion about broader pedagogical issues related to the development of multiliteracies. As part of the action research cycle, teachers developed 'learning stories' and portfolios about each of their focus children. Teachers also generated reflective and summary/analysis documents in relation to their inquiries and their developing understandings about multi-literacies in action.

During the course of their inquiries, teachers identified specific professional learning needs, and in response to these professional development sessions were developed. These sessions provided further opportunities for reflection and the integration of theory and practice.

Data, evidence, analysis and knowledge creation

An important consideration for this research was how to generate new knowledge that was created on the basis of empirical data that was analysed in a rigorous and valid way, which identified 'signposts for action' that practitioners regarded as relevant and accessible (Anderson and Heer 1999; Conners 1991; Erlandson *et al.* 1993; Hopkins 1987; Stake 1987). As part of the collaborative practitioner research process, teachers synthesized the documentation they produced, learning from their actions taken during their inquiries and from student artefacts that were the result of their teaching. In dialogue with the coordinating researchers, they interrogated the multiliteracies framework and identified examples from practice that enabled more grounded analysis, interpretation and theorizing. As primary teachers joined the project, collaborative analysis and interpretation were encouraged between teachers. Preschool teachers began to assume the role of the coordinating researchers, asking reflective and probing questions that caused their primary colleagues to begin rethinking their literacy and technology practices. Insights from the teacher researcher analysis and reflection shared during the RACs were compiled into a collective response by the mentors and returned to teachers for 'member checking' (Erlandson *et al.* 1993).

Our knowledge creation process was based on data and evidence gathered through what Wolcott (1992: 19) proposed as being a full range of data-gathering techniques:

> Experiencing, with emphasis on sensory data, particularly watching

and listening; enquiring, in which the researcher's role becomes more intrusive than that of a 'mere observer'; and examining, in which the research makes use of materials prepared by others.

For our purposes this consisted of:

- *Classroom observations:* Both teachers and coordinating researchers engaged in classroom observation with a more specific emphasis on the focus children.
- *Reflections:* Both teachers and coordinating researchers developed and shared reflections about practice, pedagogy and children's developing facility with multiliteracies and ICT.
- *Group dialogue and discussion:* The coordinating researchers facilitated structured discussions to explore teachers' learning processes, gain feedback on their specific inquiries and how these were impacting professional learning, and discuss changes that were occurring.
- *Individual interviews:* Individual interviews with teachers were conducted as part of the classroom visit cycle of observation.
- *National reference group:* A reference group of professionals and researchers from both within and outside the study was gathered together to enable a final collaborative analysis and discussion of findings.
- *Literature:* Literature related to multiliteracies, early childhood education and use of ICT was provided to the group for discussion and reflection. Research literature was accessed by the coordinating researchers and used to position and strengthen our approach.
- *Documentation:* Teachers and coordinating researchers documented practice, photographed artefacts and children engaged in literacy and learning practices, minutes of meetings and summaries of discussions in addition to their reflections.

Ely *et al.* (1991) emphasize that data analysis should be continuous and progressive from the beginning of data collection. Data analysis took place progressively during our research, with coordinating researchers meeting annually to collate findings from the three states, then sharing this and facilitating local interrogation and dialogue with teacher researchers. Hammersley and Atkinson (1995) stress it is important to devise ways of developing and testing the ideas that emerge from the analysis. Data that appears to be most central to the analysis need to be worked on with a view to clarifying meaning and exploring their relations.

The project incorporated collaborative analysis and validation with the teacher researchers as well as individual analyses. The overall analysis was 'member checked' by the teacher researchers (Lincoln and Guba 1985). We felt that this strategy enabled a more holistic picture within both individual and successive narratives to be kept in focus. In order to stay close to teachers' narratives, vignettes were distilled from the data to present 'in miniature the essence of what the researcher has seen and heard over time ... They are devices that are established through analysis and offered to provide meaning, cohesion, and colour to the presentation' (Ely *et al.* 1991: 154). These were selected at a later stage as emerging themes and propositions became apparent. Reflexivity was an important element of the methodology, which resulted in changes being made in partnership with teacher researchers. Reflexivity addressed validity concerns through application of the collaborative validation and theory building processes with teacher researchers.

Summary

At the conclusion of our research we felt that the methodology was successful in supporting and facilitating teacher learning as teachers explored a multiliteracies approach to encouraging children's literacy and learning practices using ICT. Additionally, we co-constructed a multiliteracies portrait, pedagogies and pathways framework that acts a practical guide to decision making in relation to responsive and personalized learning for children.

New forms of collaboration with teachers enable a more grounded approach to inquiry and research partnerships that produce new knowledge. In this chapter, we have focused on outlining the way we worked with teachers and children in a range of educational settings, in order to elucidate how such collaborations make new learning possible. Our ways of working with teachers aligned with the literature on effective professional learning which suggests that teachers must become researchers of their own practice and part of the theory building and knowledge construction processes. Our RACs were characterized by collaboration, dialogue, reflection and an atmosphere of mutual respect and trust.

Our research also revealed a number of enabling and constraining factors that affected the effectiveness of our collaboration and partnerships. Enabling factors included the provision of release time for teachers to engage in dialogue and reflection; opportunities to visit one another's classrooms; supportive school leadership; partnerships and support of coordination researchers; responsive opportunities for skill development and professional reading. Teachers reported an increased sense of professionalism as a result of their participation in the project and several volunteered to make presentations of their work to others.

Challenges to or constraints on our research design included those involved with attrition; losing children to new schools; teachers of the focus children who were not willing to be involved; short-term contracts for preschool teachers which meant that they were unwilling to commit for the duration of the project. Some primary school principals did not see the value of the research and were unwilling to provide time for teacher release. It also became evident that a lack of knowledge about and access to ICT in schools raised a number of issues around educational opportunity. The increasing focus and compliance associated with alphabetic or print literacy in the form of state and national testing regimes meant that some principals and primary (early years) teachers found it difficult to embrace a broader perspective of literacy which was not part of such a viewpoint.

Overall, the teachers reported their appreciation for the research design and the opportunity to participate in practitioner research. This was especially the case with the preschool and childcare centre teachers who participated for all 3 years of the project. They could see that they had knowledge and insight about their focus children that was worth sharing and also realized that they had indeed become increasingly 'multiliterate' themselves as they continued engaging in discussion with primary school teachers. Primary (early years) teachers also indicated to us that they valued the opportunity to collaborate with others to interrogate their pedagogical practices rather than simply build up content and activities.

All co-researchers became more consciously aware about the ways in which knowledge of the diverse lifeworlds of children can be used to inform and enrich the curriculum and the importance of focusing on the strengths of the child, their preferred ways of learning and making sense of the world and the 'funds of knowledge' that they bring to any learning relationship. The need to provide children with multiliterate pathways to print as well as the opportunity to develop as multiliterate young people became evident as an equity and access issue.

The research and learning approach, where coordinating researchers used a conceptual framework to analyse the evidence and data and then share this with the teachers for reflection, interrogation and synthesis enabled the creation of a practical framework to guide pedagogical and practice outcomes. This is presented in Chapter 7.

Finally, our methodology has implications for future approaches to professional learning that might lead to sustainable changes in pedagogical practice. These included opportunities for participants to interrogate:

- the foundational knowledge and skills/strategies we aimed to pursue in partnership with teachers
- the relational understandings and meaning-making we pursued
- the reflective/critical aspect of our approach
- the creative dimension of our work together.

This chapter has identified how crucial the relationship and role of teachers was in translating theory into practice, and vice versa, in early childhood settings, with particular reference to the use of a range of ICT. It became apparent that the longitudinal nature of the study and opportunity for subsequent teachers to form partnerships and relationships with one another, identified and challenged their different perceptions about children's abilities. It caused teachers to question their pedagogical practices, move away from superficial interpretations of children's responses and look at ways of enabling children to build on their relative strengths and learning preferences so as to maximize their learning potential. Teachers deferred from making judgements about the children and each other, and became more focused on the inquiry process and how to create solutions to problems and issues that arose as a result of their daily work. In this way, we felt that we achieved some of the emancipatory outcomes of critical action research, particularly where teachers identified successful learning pathways for children who traditionally struggle to experience success in school. Teachers also reported the personal value in being challenged to look at children through different lenses and to subsequently challenge their preconceptions and construct a different image of children in terms of their competence in a multiliterate context.

Hannah was initially sceptical about the use of computers in a preschool setting:

> One of the most difficult things I faced was how to use this teaching tool. How am I going to teach the children about it when I don't know anything about it? I spent hours reading and playing with the Young Explorer. I was still unfamiliar with it and was very hesitant in using it confidently with the children. For a while there we ignored it and avoided it. Then one day I thought to myself, 'what is it that is stopping me using this with the children?' I realized then that it was my own fear of it. Not knowing enough about it, not being able to observe it, plan, prepare and implement it! So I thought that this is what I should be sharing with the children. I should tell them it is new to me, that I don't know much about it. So together we should learn about it and that I would need them to help me as well as I would help them. Let's explore and learn together as we go!!! The children were fantastic and they felt so good when they found out something that I didn't. They too were being the big preschool teacher!

She participated in the research project for all 3 years and her ability to carefully and insightfully question her primary school colleagues about their practices and views about the focus children, without judgement, had the effect of causing them to rethink their own practice in light of her queries. She remained interested in her focus children's journey through primary school and continued to challenge herself, both in her own classroom and by contributing regionally to conferences and exhibitions. One of her final reflections illustrates the growth and depth of her learning and her capacity to interpret and theorize about her own practice:

> An absolute wealth of knowledge has been acquired by not only the children but also me as a practising teacher. The most critical aspects to remember are the importance of 'exploration' and 'opportunity' to experience various technological mediums. I could never imagine how many enriched learning opportunities could be explored using a variety of technology. Children have discovered so many more open-ended opportunities that I would not have expected. The social interactions, communication and creativity that have developed have been exceptionally important for all children, but in particular my focus children. These children have had the opportunity to use technology as a tool to help express themselves and communicate more effectively. I feel that all children need to be exposed to a balance of traditional play experiences and a good variety of technological equipment to enhance overall learning and development. The idea of multiliteracies is a crucial element of early childhood education. Technology has just become a part of our everyday program just as water play and painting has. In many ways having such visual aides facilitates and accelerates learning for all children, particularly for NESB [non-English speaking background] children or children who have not yet grasped great language or social skills.

Our broad aim of identifying effective pedagogies to guide learning and literacy supported by the use of ICT in early childhood centres and classrooms was realized through our collaborative interrogation and analysis of issues with teachers. Together, we were able to investigate and construct an approach using ICT in early childhood that was guided by a belief in and valuing of the importance and relevance of multiliteracies. This was necessary to ensure new learning in early childhood addressed the needs and diversity of children who came to school with many different backgrounds and experiences. By using the principles embedded in a pedagogy of multiliteracies to guide the use of ICT, teachers and children found ways to harness the technologies for their own purposes and expand their communication opportunities. This is explored further in Chapters 3 and 4.

3 Becoming multiliterate in contemporary times

Introduction

In Chapter 1, we considered new learning and suggested that it requires us to rethink and reconceptualize the learning opportunities for children in our schools in order to assist them to cope with the rigours of their daily lives in contemporary times. Inherent to being able to function effectively in the twenty-first century is the ability to be multiliterate and work with multiple modalities of information and communication systems. In this chapter, we describe what this means and provide examples from our work with teachers to illustrate how it can be achieved in early childhood pre-school centres and classrooms. Throughout this book we use the context of multiliteracies as the cornerstone for our rethinking of learning in the early childhood years. In doing so we link home and school practices around literacy and communication and reflect on how new technologies impact on the ways in which we communicate and interpret a range of multimodal texts. For many of us, this will require a shift in values and subsequently the kind of learning opportunities we create for students in school and early childhood settings. Our views of literacy must necessarily include an expansion to new literacies and multiliteracies if children are to be adequately prepared to engage in the social and literate practices of contemporary times.

Our view of becoming multiliterate in contemporary times is necessarily informed by and able to connect to the thinking and work of others. In this chapter, we outline what we believe are important contributions that make a strong case for rethinking learning and literacy and then present our findings which add to this debate and rapidly increasing body of knowledge. We discuss what it means to 'become multiliterate' both from a theoretical perspective and using data from our work with early childhood teachers. Cummins (2005) noted that there was a lack of grounded research to support the theoretical constructs that existed in this area. Accordingly, one of the outcomes of our work was the construction of a framework of practice that used the language of teachers, work of children and theoretical constructs consistent with calls to rethink literacy learning in schools and early childhood settings. Together with the work of Pahl and Rowsell (2006) and the Children of the New Millennium research project (Hill *et al.* 2002), our work adds to the growing body of empirical data that links theory and practice to provide strong evidence for change.

Changing views of literacy

Luke (2006) argues that it is necessary to reconceptualize literacy as the acquisition of a 'malleable repertoire of practices' rather than simply acquiring a set of literacy skills. He states:

> Learning to be literate is like learning to be an artisan in a guild, to play an instrument in an ensemble, like acquiring a craft within a community whose art and forms of life are dynamic, rather than a robotic acquisition and automization of core skills.
>
> (2006: xi)

Traditionally, the literate practices of schools have emphasized reading, writing, listening and speaking. The advent of ICT requires an expansion of this focus to include the interplay between visual, aural, spatial and gestural modes of communication (New London Group 1996). The Children of the New Millennium research project (Hill *et al.* 2002) identified the importance of connecting emergent and early literacy to the multimodal context of multi-literacies. Our own work supports this notion and also suggests that we need to build on the 'funds of knowledge' (Moll *et al.* 1992) that children bring to early childhood settings in order to connect with children's lifeworld experiences so that we are able to engage and extend their capabilities. We discovered that this was often more easily achieved in preschool settings where teachers were more likely to adopt a multiliteracies perspective and that this enabled them to more effectively notice and build on children's existing literate practices and literacy identities in appropriate ways.

Young children are already predisposed to communicate and make meaning through multiple modes, as observation in any preschool or kindergarten will show. However, when they come to school it becomes apparent that traditional forms of print literacy are privileged and promoted in a range of activities that characterize the 'literacy hour'. To some extent this can be linked to accountability regimes in which tests of literacy and numeracy rely on historically devised items that constituted the old basics of reading, writing and arithmetic. Yet although many teachers and curriculum developers are aware of the rapid technological advances that have occurred in recent times, they are yet to link these with a contemporary view of literacy.

In our study, we asked both preschool and primary school teachers to share with us their conceptualization of literacy from the outset of the research project. It was immediately apparent that the preschool teachers began with a multimodal view of literacy that had a broader communicative intent. For example, one preschool teacher who attended our first RAC said:

> Literacy is a hard thing to define. I suppose the traditional idea is reading and writing, but I believe it is broader than that. Literacy to me is being able to communicate a message or information and there are many different ways of doing this. There is written, oral, body language, photographs, other visuals like posters, charts, graphs, symbols (what 3-year-old doesn't recognize the golden arches?). Then there are subject-specific languages, each subject area has its own jargon and language.
>
> (Preschool teacher, RAC meeting)

In contrast, during our conversations with primary school teachers in the second year, it became evident that they possessed a narrower view of literacy that was essentially print-based. In another research circle a primary school teacher indicated her view:

> I think literacy is about enabling children to communicate, gain information/understandings about the world effectively through reading, writing, speaking and listening. Share/express their own ideas, interests and enjoy the experience.
>
> (Primary school teacher, RAC meeting)

Children are growing up immersed in multimodal symbol forms at home and in their community, with the increasing prevalence of computers providing them with access to 'symbol machines' and 'multiple sign systems' (State of South Australia, Department of Education and Children's Services and University of South Australia 2006: 6). Thus becoming multiliterate in contemporary times requires educators to consider literacy through the lens of semiotic theory. Semiotics provides the means for a consideration of multiple sign systems and can assist us to understand the underlying processes involved when we consider graphic/symbolic representations. The work of Labbo (1996) considers both the individual's cognitive capacity in their interpretation of symbols as well as the broader context in which they occur and influence interactions and thinking. This enables a rich understanding of the ways in which meanings are made and goals accomplished using 'semiotic resources' which can include oral language, visual symbols, music, constructions in space and gestures (Kress and van Leeuwen, 2001; State of South Australia, Department of Education and Children's Services and University of South Australia 2006).

Multimodality

People communicate through multiple modes (linguistic, visual, aural, gestural and spatial) and draw on a variety of personal resources and contextual understandings to do so. How often have we heard the statement that 80% of oral communication is making sense of the non-verbal? Children are also growing up saturated in multimodal information environments which mediate and shape their linguistic competence (Pahl and Rowsell 2006). Pahl and Rowsell identified such competence as including:

- ways of taking in information from the environment
- ways of manipulating symbols and systems
- ways of playing and making sense of the world
- ways of developing a sense of self and communicative norms.

Print literacy has long held a privileged position in our school literacy programmes despite the rising dominance of other modes of communication as affordability and access to digital technologies increase. Schools are still grappling with the implications of voice, image, movement and gesture now being able to be easily recorded and transferred via digital technologies. This can be likened to the impact that the invention of the printing press initially had on print literacy. Contemporary technological environments necessitate that we no longer pay lip-service to the modes of communication other than print. There is a need for rigour in developing children's facility with all communication modes, in 'reading' and producing multimodal 'texts', in exploring the best way to represent and communicate ideas powerfully, and in reading the 'world' as well as the word (Freire 1973). These are necessary aspects of contemporary literacy practice and are discussed with examples in more detail in the next chapter.

Each communication mode brings with it a different foundational base of conventions, logic and organization, so becoming multiliterate requires the refinement of skills, knowledge and understanding of the foundational underpinnings of each mode. The following 'design elements' of multimodal texts have been broken down into possible foundational components (Healy and Honan 2004: 21; State of South Australia, Department of Education and Children's Services and University of South Australia 2006: 11):

Design element	Component				
Linguistic design	Vocabulary	Metaphor	Structure	Delivery	Modality
Aural design	Voice	Music	Sound effects		
Spatial design	Ecosystem	Geographical	Architectural		
Visual	Colour	Perspective	Vectors	Foreground	Background
Gestural	Behaviour-action	Sensuality	Body control	Emotion	Kinesics

This, however, still only leads to a functional or technical literacy. To become literate in the broad sense, children must also be able to make relational meanings, critique both the form and function of texts and produce their own texts using their newly developed skills and knowledge to transform language and ideas for their own creative purposes.

There is now a significant body of work on multimodality (Finnegan 2002; Hodge and Kress 1988; Jewitt 2006; Jewitt and Kress 2003; Kress and van Leeuwen 1996, 2001; Martin and Veel 1998; Martinec 2000; O'Toole 1994; van Leeuwen 1999). Jewitt (2006: 40) notes that 'all texts are multimodal and modes are always interconnected in a text'. Even the meaning and message of the printed word is affected by colour, size, font and placement. By exploring the conventions and designs of each mode, then considering the impact these have in relation to one another, we develop children's ability to accurately read or produce meaning in the form of multimodal texts. Each mode has a system of conventions and resources that assist communication and meaning making, and as students 'take up these resources, transform them and design meaning with them' (Jewitt 2006: 40) they advance down a pathway to becoming multiliterate.

Rethinking literacy

Luke and Freebody (1999, 2000) created a four-resources model for literacy that addressed the following key questions:

- What does it mean to be a literate member of contemporary society?
- What types of practice should a balanced school literacy programme include?

They believed that all learners needed to be proficient in four interrelated and interdependent dimensions of language use and over time have 'stretched' their model to try and incorporate multimodal texts:

- code-breaking resources – an ability to 'crack the code' of texts by understanding their underlying 'fundamental features'
- text-participating resources – understanding and composing meaningful written, visual and spoken texts by drawing on available knowledge and experiences; being able to make inferences about these connections
- text-using resources – understanding the social relations around texts, the social functions they perform and the social action that can be accomplished by using particular texts and text forms
- text-analysing resources – interrogating and critiquing texts beyond the level of content or mechanics to identify particular points of view and the dialogic relationship with the reader.

Luke and Freebody's (1999) view of literacy linked the resources of the individual (in terms of their repertoire of capabilities) with their social practices. This involved successful engagement in a family of practices or actions that they 'performed, negotiated, and achieved in everyday classroom and community contexts'. They also promoted a dynamic view of literacy in which practices were 'being redeveloped, recombined, and articulated in relation to one another on an ongoing basis'. In this way, their view of literacy was viewed as active and social, with 'substantive and visible, dynamic and fluid practices undertaken by human agents in social contexts'.

Lankshear and Knobel (2004) critiqued this view of literacy as a 'stretch' which cannot adequately account for multimodal texts while remaining an extrapolation of what we know about reading and writing print. Instead, they argue for new mindsets to address the interfaces between literacy, technology and social practices and call for a range of new literacies to be incorporated into education. This notion is supported by the work of Kress (2003) who argues that representation and meaning making undergo significant changes in logic and organization when we shift from a linguistic print environment to contexts of multimodal communication and information exchange. For example, speech and language are governed by the logics of time and chronological sequence. Images, in contrast, are governed by a logic of space and function where meaning can be constructed from placement, size, colour and shape. Kress suggested that the world described or told is vastly different from the world that is shown (see also Lankshear and Knobel 2004).

Leu (1996, 2000a, 2000b, 2002) also emphasizes that we can undermine children's ability to succeed in the future if we only emphasize the reading of traditional book literacies in a multimedia world. In particular, he examines how the Internet has brought vast array of new reading and writing opportunities for children of all ages, with new forms of social and cultural interactions able to take place.

Additionally, Marsh (2004) considered the importance of identifying children's technoliteracy practices prior to entering school as part of any analysis of children's emergent literacy. When the literacy practices that children are engaging in at home and in their local community are examined, children can be seen to actively demonstrate a complex range of contemporary literacy skills, knowledge and understandings. She actively challenges the notion of 'pre-readers' and 'pre-writers' and calls for the communicative competencies that children develop from birth to be acknowledged.

The call for educators to consider the assets that children bring to formal settings requires a consideration of the strengths of their communicative and literate practices in home, school and community settings. This was particularly evident in our own work in disadvantaged areas of large metropolitan cities. In order to document and capture this information so that it could be used in the planning process, we worked with teachers to create children's portraits that included a description of their physical, cultural, social and emotional life experiences. In this way, teachers were able to construct a richer profile of the child as a literacy learner and consequently identify more personalized and successful pathways to literacy, including print literacy. We recognized that there are multiple pathways to acquiring print literacy and the social practices of literacy. Our research indicated that children were able to more successfully develop their literacy identities and practices in classrooms that took a multiliteracies perspective than in classrooms where the emphasis on print literacy devalued other modes of communication. Such multiliteracies classrooms emphasized:

- finding an effective literacy pathway for each child
- utilizing and building upon children's preferred ways of communicating and making sense of the world
- acknowledging children's 'funds of knowledge' (Moll *et al.* 1992)
- providing opportunities for and making links between multimodal communication of ideas.

What do we therefore mean by 'becoming multiliterate'? The New London Group (1996) used the term 'multiliteracies' to link print, visual and audio texts that they noted were increasingly become more culturally diverse. The term also related to the communicative skills of speaking, writing and reading (Hagood 2000). The *raison d'être* for a new term was based on the premise that making meaning from texts was become increasingly complex as a result of major changes in our social world in the latter part of the twentieth century. They used two instances to support this view. Firstly, the way in which mass media permeate everything we see and do is essentially carried out in linguistic and visual modes. This means that we need to be able to read these effectively and derive our own meanings about their effectiveness and purpose. Secondly, everyday actions require that we coordinate and make sense of linguistic meaning in written texts together with other modalities such as the spatial. In this way a visit to a shopping mall requires that we are able to negotiate signs that are both written and visual as well as to understand the spatial architecture of the building. They contend that 'All meaning making is multimodal. All written text is also visually designed' (New London Group 1996: 81) and further that spoken language is 'a matter of audio design as much as it is a matter of linguistic design understood as grammatical relationships' (1996: 81).

The original work noted that since the interplay between the modes will vary in importance between cultures, pedagogical practices should be constructed that support meaning making in diverse ways. The pedagogy of multiliteracies (New London Group 1996) was based on four key ideas for teaching and learning. They are regarded as components that are interrelated and should not be regarded as linear or stages, since they may occur simultaneously. They are: situated practice, overt instruction, critical framing and transformed practice.

Situated practice involves immersion in experience, drawn either from students' varied lifeworlds or from new experiences which have some purchase on student subjectivity. This aspect builds upon the tradition of experiential learning. It recognizes that learning is highly situated in a social and cultural sense and that learning must operate within a 'zone of proximal development' (Vygotsky 1978).

Overt instruction involves systematic, analytic and conscious understandings. It requires the introduction of an explicit, abstract, conceptual language to describe the underlying structures of meaning. Vygotsky describes the epistemological basis of this process in terms of a shift from the world of complex, analogical thinking (meanings which make sense only because they are situated in experience) to the world of generalizable concepts, transferable from one cultural or lifeworld setting to another (Luria 1976; Vygotsky 1962).

Critical framing requires the interpretation of the social and cultural context of knowledge. It necessitates that learners reflect on their work from a variety of critical perspectives and consider, for example, the purpose and function of a piece of knowledge.

Transformed practice relates to the transfer in meaning-making practice, which puts knowledge to work in new contexts or cultural sites. This perspective builds upon a tradition of applied learning, or learning by doing, in which learning occurs through a process of transfer of generalizable knowledge from one setting to another (Luke 1994).

These features have been built on in a variety of ways. For example, in the Children of the New Millennium project (Hill *et al.* 2002) a framework for considering the nature and complexity of young children's learning to become multiliterate was created so that teachers could use it as a source for their planning to ensure that they were able to consider the various dimensions of meaning. Originally called the *concepts of information and communications technology framework*, it consisted of four integrated dimensions for considering how to become multiliterate that incorporated the use of ICT: functional, meaning making, critical and transformative. The functional dimension described the basic use of ICT, that is, being able to work with multimodal texts such as computers, turn them on and recognize that they use icons and symbols for different purposes. The meaning-making dimension looked at how the learner comes to understand how different text types and new technologies work and the subsequent meanings that are derived from them. It also involves a consideration of the ways in which texts and messages can be constructed to promote specific or desired meanings via knowing the function and form of various texts. The *critical* was concerned with how the learner realizes that messages will be different based on how the interpretation of meaning is made and that this will vary across context, time and lifeworlds. Finally, the *transformative* dimension was concerned with applying what is learned in new contexts for new purposes.

The framework was used by teachers for planning and observing learning in their various settings. After some time they came to realize that it was effective since prior to its introduction they had tended to focus on the functional aspect but were now prompted to extend their range of pedagogies into the other dimensions. The framework was adapted and became a multiliteracies map (see Table 3.1) so that teachers were able to incorporate it into their work to observe how children developed as:

- functional users of multiliteracies texts
- makers of meaning from a range of multimodal materials/texts
- critical interpreters who were able to analyse multimodal texts effectively
- transformers or producers of new texts on the basis of their interactions and meaning making in prior contexts.

Table 3.1   The multiliteracies map (Hill *et al.* 2002: 146)

Functional user	Meaning maker
• Locating, code breaking; using letters, signs, icons	• Understanding multimodal meanings
• Selecting and operating equipment	• Understanding purpose of text and text form
• Moving between media: oral, paper, cameras, videos, computers	• Connecting to prior knowledge
Critical analyser	**Transformer**
• Analysing discourses	• Using skills and knowledge in new ways
• Analysing issues of equity, power and position	• Designing texts
• Choosing appropriate mode	• Producing new texts

In our own work we were aware of the usefulness of the multiliteracies map and earlier work by O'Rourke (2005) – see Table 3.2 – but some significant differences emerged as a result of our research with teachers, which necessitated a rethinking of each component.

Essentially there are three key aspects to becoming multiliterate that we address:

- multimodality – being able to read the layers of meaning in multi-modal forms of communication and 'texts', including linguistic, visual, aural, spatial and gestural modes;
- social and cultural practices in contemporary times – developing a sense of self and repertoire of capabilities and understandings that enable meaning making and participation in contemporary social and cultural practices;
- acquiring knowledge for contemporary living – learning to learn, be, live and know in order to lead personally fulfilling lives, contribute to family life and engage in local and global communities.

This is described more fully in Table 3.3, which was developed in collaboration with teacher researchers (O'Rourke 2003, 2005).

The four dimensions of literacy and learning identified above that form the foundation of our framework – relational, foundational, critical and creative – are applicable regardless of the communication mode. The modes of communication listed are the common forms of communication used in pre-school and primary school settings, such as language and print, still and moving images, music, performance, gestures and constructions in space, but not all are privileged to the same degree. The dimensions of literacy and learning also articulate broader pedagogical, planning and assessment considerations

Table 3.2 O'Rourke's (2005) multiliteracies framework for learning and literacy

Relational dimension	**Foundational dimension**
• Make relational connections of a personal, local and global nature and account for contexts that are shaped and influenced by the social, cultural, political and historical	• Read and use the underpinning skills, knowledge, structures and conventions of different text forms and technologies
Critical dimension	**Creative dimension**
• Reflect, analyse, critique and give feedback about both the form and focus of various texts	• Produce texts that develop and communicate their ideas and understandings effectively and powerfully

Table 3.3 Dimensions of literacy* (O'Rourke 2005)

	Modes of communication				
Dimensions of learning and literacy	Print and linguistic e.g. oral and printed word, different languages	Visual e.g. still and moving images: photographs, graphics, drawings, animation, video	Spatial and gestural e.g. performance, body language, constructions in space	Aural e.g. voice, music, sound effects	Mixed mode
Relational dimension	Drawing on life experience and contextual knowledge (e.g. social, cultural, historical, political context). Creating meaning, making sense, making connections. Exploring alternative ways of knowing and seeing, developing understandings of the world. Identifying what is worth pursuing in a human sense				
Foundational dimension	Foundational skills, knowledge and text conventions. Techniques, principles, composition strategies, spelling, grammar, technical, editing and production skills etc.				
Critical dimension	Critical thinking and analysis. Reflecting on what worked, why, how it could be better. Identifying different interpretations and meanings and what influences are at work. Noticing the dominant. Noticing what is missing. Identifying ways forward and how to improve. Audience considerations – how well was the intention communicated?				
Creative dimension	Using new learning and imagination to transform and extend existing practices, generate new questions and ideas; design, realize and communicate ideas and understandings, generate outcomes that are original and of value, use judgement to assess and refine creative work				

* This framework builds on the work of Cope and Kalantzis (2000), Fisher and Williams (2004), Kalantzis and Cope (2001), Kalantzis *et al.* (2005), Lankshear and Snyder (2000) and New London Group (1996).

for teachers as they identify how best to expand the literacy repertoire of practices in their classrooms.

The *relational* dimension is a reminder that literacy is not a simple technical endeavour. It is shaped and influenced by the individual meaning maker and communicator drawing on their knowledge and life experience. This includes their general knowledge base, knowledge of others, reading situations and contexts. It also refers to the little considered affective or emotional aspect of communication, for example when music is used to create a mood or feeling associated with a message.

The *foundational* dimension refers to the particular knowledge and skills that need to be taught, accessed and practised in order to become proficient.

While huge emphasis has been placed on the foundational skills associated with reading and writing and, to an important but lesser extent, on listening and speaking, the foundational conventions associated with visual, aural, spatial and gestural modes have often been left to chance or tacit learning. To become literate, children must develop conscious practice and the associated vocabulary if they are to develop the facility to critique and create with rigour.

The *critical* dimension of literacy and learning provides opportunities for critical engagement where students are encouraged to use higher-order thinking, reflection and analysis. This means encouraging children to reflect on the content of their work, its relevance to audiences, and the appropriateness of the mode of communication they have used to exhibit their knowledge and ideas. At a more complex level it also involves an examination of power relationships and relative benefits. For teachers, it means reviewing children's work in light of the design of the learning environment – physically, socially and culturally – and the extent to which students give and receive feedback, revisit their initial ideas and reshape their texts with such feedback in mind. Teachers' ability to question effectively, provide scaffolding and support to stretch students in their thinking is also a contributing factor to how well the critical dimension of literacy is developed.

The *creative* dimension provides opportunities to genuinely assess how well the other dimensions of literacy have been assimilated as they are adapted, adopted and innovated upon when a child transforms what they have learned for their own purposes. This is where the expression, testing and elaboration of ideas take place, with learners creating their own opportunities as they manipulate, reconstruct and transform language and situations meaningfully – 'something new is created and there is significant change or "transformation" in the pupil' (Jeffrey and Craft 2004: 2).

This framework provides a *crosswalk* with the pedagogy of multiliteracies (New London Group 1996) and also links with the more recent work on learning by design (Kalantzis and Cope 2008) which conceptualizes pedagogy as knowledge in action. *Situated practice* is aligned with experiencing the known and the new; *overt instruction* with conceptualizing by naming and theorizing; *critical framing* with analysing functionally and critically; and *transformed practice* into acting appropriately and creatively (see Figure 3.1).

Social and cultural practices in contemporary times

Engaging in social and cultural practices involves drawing on past knowledge as well as making new connections and contextual associations. It requires reflection and critical analysis so that determinations can be made as to the best way to communicate ideas or make sense of experiences. New

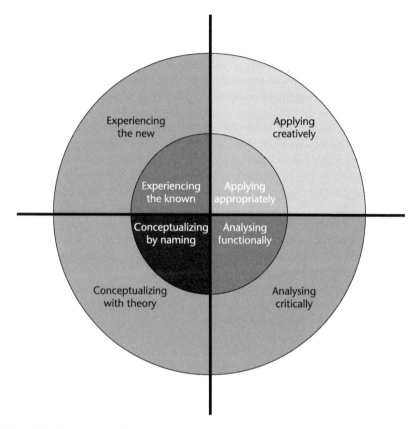

Figure 3.1 Learning by design (from Kalantzis and Cope 2008).

contemporary tools and social practices require rethinking as to what constitutes literacy in contemporary times.

Luke (2006: xii) notes that schools and education systems are struggling to
keep up with the need to transition from:

- producing 'monocultural, print children'
- curriculum practices that are designed to 'reproduce relatively static
  and stable disciplinary knowledge'
- cultivating 'local and often narrowly parochial identities and national
  ideologies'.

In the next chapter we discuss the case of Alex, whose preschool teacher
identified his preference for communicating and expressing his ideas through
the aural mode. In one activity, for example, he was involved in sequencing

and matching instruments to sounds, and then later creating his own composition for his friends to follow. Alex was fluent in this mode of operation and the communication of ideas around it.

Twelve months later, when Alex's primary teacher joined our research project, she initially expressed serious concerns about his literacy capacity and suggested that he did not seem very interested in print. He was very reluctant to read or write at school. Six months into his primary schooling, he was demonstrating very few signs of 'literacy' according to print literacy conventions. When his primary teachers had the opportunity to read the preschool learning stories, they were somewhat shocked and thought that he sounded like a different child. They were not seeing the concentration and motivation to engage that were clear in the learning story. His teachers decided to incorporate more multiliterate learning opportunities, particularly the use of aural activities and music, into their practice. Within 12 months Alex had found his 'pathway to print' through opportunities to express and explore his ideas through music, singing and dance. His story is elaborated further in Chapter 4.

Thus, incorporating a multiliteracies perspective into new learning in early childhood means valuing the diversity of children and their learning approaches and being sensitive and aware of their experiences beyond school.

A multiliteracies perspective of literacy that encourages children to engage with different modalities, cultural identities and relational meanings addresses some of Luke's major concerns. Another example to illustrate this point is the prevalence of using European fairy tales in early childhood literacy programmes. In countries such as the UK, Australia, USA and Canada, children are exposed to these stories far more often than the fairy tales of Chinese, Vietnamese, Arabic and African heritage. This is despite immigration patterns that have seen an increase in the population of people of these backgrounds. We do children a disservice by not attending to the literature we provide them with access to and the subsequent impact on their literacy identities. We therefore need to be sensitive about the overuse of traditional European fairy tales and also attend to the 'tales' from the ethnic and cultural groups in our classes.

The following vignette, based on an observation in one of the primary school classrooms of one of our focus children during his first year there, took place 6 months into the school year and illustrates the above concern:

> When I arrived, Gemma [teacher] was reading a story (Puss-in-Boots) to her class. After the story, the children were asked to do their group work with one activity centred around DeBono's black hat. The unit of work was based around fairy tales and one group had to write about the bad things or problems in Snow White.

The children in this group were from diverse backgrounds (Sudan, Vietnam, China, Somalia, Middle East) and several seemed stumped by the black hat activity. One little girl, Ming, whose family had emigrated from China, was very reluctant to commit anything to paper. 'You write for me!!' she demanded peremptorily. When asked if she knew the story of Snow White she said no. Her friend, Atifa, reminded her, 'you know, the one with the naughty queen.' I asked them what they thought the problems were or what was bad in the story. Atifa identified the apple. I asked Ming if she knew what shape an apple was and she indignantly told me that she knew how to draw an apple and turned over her sheet and proceeded to draw one. She still didn't want to put any marks on the worksheet. I noticed that the top said they could draw or write and suggested to the girls that they just draw the problems. Atifa responded 'No, we only do that afterwards' suggesting that children were already learning that print was more highly valued as a communication mode than the visual. Also, the emphasis on print and a story that was foreign in both a cultural and familial sense seemed to be causing Ming a loss of confidence and willingness to take risks when it came to responding to the Snow White worksheet.

(Classroom observation, October)

Engaging in social and cultural practices involves drawing on past knowledge and making new connections and contextual associations. It requires reflection and critical analysis so that determinations can be made as to the best way to communicate ideas or make meaning from various forms of communication. New contemporary tools and social practices require rethinking as to what constitutes foundational knowledge, skills, conventions of practice and the underlying systems and structures of the various modes of literate practices. This means broadening what is valued as 'literacy' to encompass the various modes and also attending more closely to providing children with a balance of foundational, relational, critical and creative literacy and learning opportunities. In this way, children will have the opportunity to learn about relevant traditions, make links and connections to their own experiences and cultural heritage and be encouraged to express and develop their ideas in relation to new possibilities.

In another example from our project one of the case study children, called Jack, was quick to pick up on which literate practices were valued in his first year at school and he worked hard to develop his social capital in this regard. His preschool and home social practices were different from his school practices. In his preschool year, Jack chose to play and explore his ideas through the full range of modalities. Six months into his first year of school, Jack was articulating his literacy identity by citing his interests as:

I like Maths, especially sums, and I also like reading. We get a book for each night after school. I like to read my readers.

(Jack, age 5)

He had worked out that there was social capital in developing a facility with print and had shaped himself to align with this. The values of home and school, in his case, were well-aligned, with both parents interested in and supportive of his reading and writing, and both assisting in the classroom as helpers. Discussions with his parents revealed that Jack's home literacy practices were more multiliterate in nature than his school practices.

At home, Jack loved number puzzles and construction such as Mobilo and Lego. He was attempting to build a Lego computer. His father was a musician, and Jack showed his interest in music by choosing a CD each night to go to bed. They would often have a discussion about the cover of the CD and how the music made Jack feel. Jack also went on the Internet at home and liked to check his mother's emails. His agency in relation to his home literate practices was much more evident than in his school literate practices. Interestingly, when Jack was asked to explain what he was doing in a Web Quest, his teacher prompted him several times, with use of the Internet in this case clearly a result of instigation by his teacher. In contrast, at home he was instigating Internet use, with the adult providing guided interaction (Plowman and Stephen 2007).

Thus Jack was very quick to pick up on the social and cultural capital that was valued at school and in effect was 'censoring' his interests to better adapt to the highly valued practices of reading, writing and mathematics. At school, he channelled his energies into these practices, while at home he continued a broader repertoire of interests and activities that were valued by his parents. To enable a view of Jack as 'literate' therefore required information from his parents to genuinely construct a portrait of his literacy practices. We address this further in Chapter 7 in our recommendation for a portrait of children to be developed, particularly as they transition from one teacher to another.

Knowledge building for contemporary living

It is important that we do not divorce the form of communication from the focus, layers, rigour and depth of thinking and ideas that are contained in any communications that we are involved in. If, as Paulo Freire suggests, becoming literate means becoming better able to read the 'world' rather than simply the word, then children must be given broader-based opportunities to 'read' and 'write' in multiple modes. Given that there has been an explosion of knowledge as the Internet has grown, it is increasingly important to pay attention to how children will acquire knowledge that is relevant in terms of understanding their world and engaging fully in the social and cultural practices of their families and local and global communities.

Learning how to learn and understand both the people and the elements in the world around them throughout life is therefore an important knowledge base that children need to develop. Gee (1999) develops this idea further, embedding literacy, learning and identity practices in the concept of discourse, or ways of knowing, doing, talking, reading and writing. These discourses are 'constructed and reproduced in social and cultural practice and interaction' (Pahl and Rowsell 2006).

Moje *et al.* (2004) argues for a 'third space' in which children's 'funds of knowledge' (Moll *et al.* 1992) are 'valued in hybrid spaces, and classroom knowledge is informed by home and community based knowledge' (Pahl and Rowsell 2006: 111). It is within this 'third space' that children are viewed as forming their literacy identities and use the cultural and social resources that they have acquired from peers, families and communities. By creating such a space, children are able to bring their knowledge base to bear on new texts, text forms and discourses that enable them to learn in a range of environments. This includes the physical, cultural, social and emotional life experiences of children.

Portraits, pedagogies and pathways

Our own work and that of other researchers has led us to create an alternative way of understanding children's literacy practices when they come to school and the subsequent assessment of and planning for personalized literacy learning. Firstly, we identified a need to construct a portrait of the individual child that encapsulated their interests, capabilities and preferred ways of communicating. This created a window to better understand the child's literacy identity and literate practices and was the beginning of forming a 'third space' where links between home, community and school social and cultural resources could be shared and used.

Following this, multiliteracies pedagogies were considered and mapped across the five modes of communication (visual, aural, gestural, linguistic and spatial) with consideration given to the dimensions of learning (relational, foundational, critical and creative). This could then be used to work out children's entry levels so that teachers could effectively scaffold their children's literacy practices. It also enabled teachers to identify the pedagogical implications for creating a personalized literacy pathway for each child.

This culminated in a pathway document that fine-tuned planning for a child's literacy development in a way that built on strengths and interests and linked to evidence and observation of children in action. By observing children's preferred ways of communicating and making sense of the world in the various environments they inhabited, teachers were better able to identify more personalized and effective pathways to literacy. Portraits, pedagogy and pathways are further explored in Chapter 7.

Summary

In this chapter, we have outlined why we believe the multiliteracies perspective is relevant and valuable in contemporary times, particularly in terms of providing a lens to re-image the child in terms of the broad-based social and cultural communicative practices that make up literacy in the twenty-first century. We believe this is necessary because the current school emphasis on print creates such a narrow definition of what it means to be literate. Thus, situating literacy as social and cultural practice helps us to understand how particular ways of knowing and communicating marginalize some children and privilege others. We explore this further in Chapters 5 and 6. We also describe the ways in which we worked with teachers to identify effective practices and pedagogies that culminated in a framework that enabled planning for and understanding the nature of multiliteracies in the early childhood years.

The pedagogy of multiliteracies (New London Group 1996) formed the basis of the work that is examined throughout this book. Jewitt and Kress (2003) strongly argue for attention to be paid to the role of new technologies and the skills they demand of children. As well as multimodality, new technologies have given rise to new 'reading paths' and texts, which can be considered as 'traces of people, contexts and implied practices' (Pahl and Rowsell 2005: 38). Literacy implies a level of consciousness (Freire 1973; Searle 1993) and the capacity to live dignified, aware, reflective and fulfilling lives.

4 Multimodality

Introduction

This chapter will explore multimodality as a key component of pedagogies of multiliteracies. Multimodality will be discussed via learning stories gathered in a variety of classrooms, each of which illustrates the pervasiveness of multiple modes of communication in the lifeworlds of young children. A multiliteracies perspective informs a way of seeing the world embracing the understanding that literacy in the twenty-first century is much more than print literacy. Access to new information and communications technologies, multimodal texts and the cultural specificity of communication forms are major influences in the lives of young children. The modalities and literacies that millennial children bring to school experiences are explored with reference to classroom practice that supports the use of multimodal texts as resources for multiliteracies learning. In assisting children to become multiliterate, teachers are able to create experiences to enhance and broaden the repertoire of modes that children utilize to make meaning. Later in this chapter we will see how teachers in different settings engaged children in multiple modes in order to strengthen their literacy.

Multimodality refers to 'a concept of communication that subsumes the written, the visual, the gestural and the tactile into one entity – a multimodal text' (Pahl and Rowsell 2005: 26). Multimodal texts often incorporate sounds (including music), written and spoken words, pictures and animations, and are most often associated with the use of computers, the Internet and software. In the twenty-first century in developed countries, young children are entering school with strong familiarity in using multiple semiotic modes. Many have their own email accounts, blogs, subscribe to lists and are at ease with the web browsers, search engines, MP3 players and console games this repertoire of experience constitutes. Thus, on entry to school, the 'funds of knowledge' (Moll *et al.* 1992) of many students extensively incorporate the technological. However, as discussed in Chapter 3, when children enter formal schooling they are often confronted with a largely monomodal literacy culture (Kress 1997). Literacy culture in school, for many children, does not reflect their multimodal lifeworlds, so that when a child enters school for the first time, there is a major shift to be made from the 'rich world of meanings made in countless ways, in countless forms, in the early years of children's lives, to the much more unidimensional world of written language' (Kress 1997: 10).

School literacy practices not only tend to be unidimensional but also place some students at increased risk of being identified as low achievers, students at educational risk, or even learning disabled. Vincent's (2005) Australian classroom-based research with 10-year-olds found that by working multi-modally within a multimedia computer environment to produce texts, students who previously struggled to communicate were experiencing success. They produced complexity in their texts and developed detailed narrative, they were also able to synthesize text with sound, graphics and animation, and Vincent (2005: 2) noted 'their struggle with communication immediately changed, as soon as they were introduced to a multimedia computer environment. The change was as sudden as it was dramatic.' Vincent (2005) advances an argument for multimodality as an important dimension of *equity* in curriculum. This position is supported notably by Daiute (1992), Kress (1997) and Stein (2003) and is further confirmed in our research, illustrated here in the cases from our research.

Multimodality affords educators an opportunity to draw on students' 'funds of knowledge' (Moll *et al.* 1992), build on their existing strengths and broaden their use of a range of modalities that reflect the complexity of their lifeworlds outside school. This enables students to generate texts in a range of ways and hence to become multiliterate. Their expertise in a new literacies framework can afford low-achieving students a different identity in the classroom.

The research reported in this book is focused quite deliberately on learning and pedagogies, with a particular emphasis on literacy learning and also creativity. Pahl and Rowsell's (2005) discussion on *affordances* is helpful in explicating how teachers may utilize pedagogies for multiliteracies to draw on student's multimodal practices. They note that 'affordances are the possibilities within texts to create meaning. Some . . . may be located in language and literacy, that is, they may be found in *written* texts. Some may, however, be *drawn*, but spatially organised to add to the writing' (2005: 127). Then students can combine their understanding of literacy in relation to reading and writing with their understanding of literacy in relation to images, as in the typical layout of a web page. In this way 'multimodality can be used in the classroom in a variety of ways to support students' learning' (2005: 127).

By introducing teachers to multiliteracies pedagogy we participated in the generation of pathways for teachers to move from simply focusing on technologies for their own sake, or on a deficit view of the child, to more inclusive starting points for the curriculum. Thinking about multimodality helped teachers to identify children's strengths and hence their pathways to multi-literacies (including print literacy). A fuller elaboration of the pathways model developed in our collaborative research with teachers will be included in Chapter 7.

Case stories

In order to exemplify the ways in which early childhood educators can harness multimodality for literacy learning and ecological assessment (Leslie and Jett-Simpson 1997), we present four examples in this chapter that are drawn from our research with children and teachers. Each case highlights the significance of pedagogy in engaging students in literacy practices. In addition, we document the pedagogical change that arises from dissatisfaction and an imperative to try something new in order to 'reach' students who are not restricted to one modality of learning. We include these stories to demonstrate how redesigning curriculum approaches and rethinking pedagogy enables teachers to access and enable a much wider range of literate practices in order for their students to demonstrate what they know and can do at school.

The first story introduces Alex, whose participation in a preschool programme enabled him to explore a range of modalities in an emergent programme. His teacher provided opportunities for Alex to express and create using gestural, spatial, aural, linguistic and visual modes using a range of media. On entry to formal schooling (i.e. Year 1), Alex's opportunities to engage multimodally were limited due to the literacy programme being predominantly print-based. Early in the year, Alex's teachers became concerned about his ability to acquire print literacy and his lack of confidence in risk taking. This story documents both Alex's journey and that of his preschool and Year 1 teachers. Our collective inquiry research enabled learning stories documented by Alex's preschool teacher to be reviewed and discussed by his Year 1 teachers. This helped them to see Alex from a new perspective and this made it possible for them to interrogate their own practices in regard to literacy acquisition. They were able to review their programme and implement a pedagogy of multiliteracies using a range of modalities to which Alex responded in a competent and confident way.

Second, the story of Cameron, an Indigenous boy who is considered 'at risk' by his teacher, is shared. Education outcomes for Indigenous students in Australia are relatively poor. In fact, the national report *Overcoming Indigenous Disadvantage* (Steering Committee for the Review of Government Service Provision 2005) notes a 'large gap between Indigenous people and the rest of the population' (2005: 1) on the following indicators:

- life expectancy at birth
- rates of disability
- school retention
- post-secondary participation and retention
- labour force participation and unemployment
- household income
- home ownership
- suicide and self-harm
- child protection notifications
- deaths from homicide
- victim rates for crime
- imprisonment, including juvenile detention.

The report identifies each of these areas as key measures of the major social and economic factors that need to improve if Indigenous people are to enjoy the same standard of living as other Australians. In recognizing the range of factors affecting quality of life, the report also identifies seven strategic areas for action, three of which relate directly to early childhood experiences and engagement at school. Hence, Cameron's story has particular significance in the chapter, since it is clear from the research reported above, and in countless other research papers, that in Australia early childhood learning has a major impact on the long-term standard of living of Indigenous students.

Cameron's story reveals how changes in pedagogy, informed by a multi-literacies framework, enabled his teacher to provide meaningful tasks for him that not only engaged him for the first time with his own learning, but also allowed him to demonstrate what he knew and could do with a personal narrative. Using his strengths in the visual mode, his interest in technologies and his home context as a starting point, Cameron's teacher ensured he progressed from the visual mode to oral language and then to print – in other words, she guided his pathway to literacy learning in a manner that was not possible in a 'standard' print-based programme. This story highlights how authentic assessment is made possible through the valuing of the social context of the child, the family and the community in which learning occurs (Fleet and Lockwood 2002). Children's home and community literacy practices are identified as 'funds of knowledge' (Moll *et al.* 1992), which form starting points for learning and teaching.

The third story documents a term-long programme utilizing dance, drama, singing and music in a metropolitan early childhood setting. In the multi-age classroom, performing arts specialists were invited to generate stories with children, utilizing combinations of gestural, aural, visual, linguistic and spatial modes. The children participating in the programme demonstrated increased engagement with storytelling and unprecedented preparedness to take risks in articulating and representing stories, ideas and feelings. As a whole-class approach, this story is instructive since it highlights the range of opportunities available for teachers to provide learning experiences in multiple modes. It shows how using a range of modes simultaneously (i.e. blends of the linguistic, gestural, spatial, visual and aural) harnesses the range of existing modalities among the students and also how to broaden their repertoire of modes in order to stimulate linguistic or alphabetic literacy.

The final story highlights multimodal learning in a popular culture context, documenting a year-long project with a group of Year 1 students who developed their own episode of *Star Wars*. A discussion of the production process as well as student outcomes is included, with reflections on pedagogy and teacher decision making to facilitate multiliteracies learning in multiple modes, with a particular emphasis on learning with ICT. In this story, a multimodal approach is utilized not only to develop the movie but also to broaden the range of modes that students draw upon in making meaning and creating narrative.

Alex: provision of multiple pathways to literacy learning

Alex in preschool

Alex loved coming to kindergarten and enjoyed activities involving blocks, cars, trains and especially the computer. He often moved very quickly on arrival to be the first to the computer:

> Alex was bursting a bubble, to have a turn on the new computer program (in this case Kid Pix). 'Can I have first turn?' he asked hopefully. He moved the mouse around, excited and having short turns on everything, a bit of stamping, drawing, backgrounds and pictures. He especially loved the blowing up of his picture and he laughed out loud.
>
> Alex had a ball with the blue stampers and loved saying the word as he experimented. Click, click, click went his fingers 'Lollies, lollies, lollies', he said. There was so much enthusiasm and lots of exploration. Alex had so much fun and enjoyed verbalizing it.
>
> (Preschool teacher, learning story)

Alex's preschool teacher, Cindy, constructed a very positive image of him as a learner. She observed his reactions to learning opportunities keenly and worked hard to understand his thinking:

> Alex explored all sorts of patterns, talking about what he had discovered. He was very keen to print out his picture [Figure 4.1] and moved quickly to the printer to watch it come out, saying 'Wow!!' I

I am ping dmincs gam pasdn2.

Terrance
5-19-06

I am playing Domic's game, Play Station 2.

Figure 4.1 Kid Pix drawing.

was curious to find out Alex's sense of imagination in more detail and asked him to tell me about his picture. 'The drink came out of the bottle. I was drinking and it spilt. I held it in two hands, but it just fell out of my hands.' As I looked at his picture, I could see his story. With Alex's great self-confidence he told an imaginative story in a logical sequence.

(Preschool teacher, learning story)

Cindy took great pleasure in discovering the interests of children in her class and following their line of thinking. Although she had clear general intentions for her preschoolers' learning, she was very open to any direction they chose to pursue and particularly placed value on imaginative and divergent thinking. In this sense, Cindy's programme was 'emergent'.

Introducing new multiliteracies activities in the preschool

Cindy was keen to explore a multiliteracies approach with Alex and, as part of her strategy, she introduced the program Super Dooper Music Looper as one way to enable Alex to extend his experience of communicating in multiple modes. This software enables children to record their own vocals, select instruments and compose songs. It is also possible to include sound effects and to email the composition to others. Cindy noted how excited Alex was when she gave him an opportunity to use this software as he exclaimed, 'I *wanted* to do this one!'

To accompany the visual and aural dimensions of the software, Cindy had also set out a range of musical instruments on the floor, including a shaker, drum, piano, triangle and tambourine. Alex eyed the musical instrument's box next to the computer with curiosity and interest.

She then selected the percussion instrument on the computer and Alex and his friend Tim listened to the sounds. She asked the boys to guess which instrument made that particular sound. Alex was very confident as he said, 'I know' and picked up the shaker and gave it a hearty shake. The boys selected the appropriate instrument on each attempt. Cindy wondered if they may have been using the pictures of the instruments on the computer as a visual clue, because some of the sounds were hard to guess or match.

Cindy then provided an opportunity for the boys to work together and play some music themselves:

> Alex beamed as he chose the drum and Evan chose the shaker. I pro-grammed the computer to play the drum and percussion sounds. Alex played the drum with vigour to the music. The boys clapped at the finish, saying 'Yeah!'
>
> The computer was then programmed to play at regular intervals. Alex played when the drum played and Tim played with the percussion. Alex kept his eyes deadlocked on the computer. When Jenny, another child, pulled a chair up Alex handed her the piano saying, 'You play the piano.' He then added the piano onto their song on the screen saying, 'You play the piano when the line goes onto the green colour.' With a knowing voice Alex instructed Jenny when to play and when to stop. Alex was so enthusiastic and what confidence at attempting new experiences! He used his listening skills, maybe with help from visual cues, to match the sounds with the instrument. He was full of concentration as he played the instrument to his music piece.
>
> I watched proudly as Alex organized a friend to join in. He set up the situation, explained the process and then guided his friend through the experience. I was also very surprised to see him add more instruments to his song just from watching me set it up.
>
> (Preschool teacher, learning story)

Alex was quick to pick up on Cindy's modelling of ways of interacting with and through technology. He readily made connections between the visual, gestural and aural modes. Cindy's programme and careful planning had afforded Alex an opportunity to be successful and to show his competence with communication.

On another occasion, Cindy had used the video camera as a device for documentation of children's learning. She roamed the classroom recording children's responses to her prompt to 'Tell me about this . . .'. When Alex had a turn with the camera, he approached one child and said, 'Sandra, watcha [*sic*] doing?' Sandra responded to him, then he moved on to the next child, saying their name and prompting them to tell him about the activity they were engaged in. Cindy was excited to see this interaction taking place, believing that the opportunity to use technology such as a video camera enhanced children's self-esteem. Alex had picked up the protocols of filming events and was acting in a 'reporter' role to document his peers' learning.

As a follow-up to these initial experiences, Cindy extended the work to include using pictures and the microphone to make a song, drawing pictures of family members, taking photographs with the digital camera and making slide shows. Children were often asked 'What music would suit your picture?' to encourage an exploration of mood and aural communication. Cindy found that Alex enjoyed expressing himself through movement to sounds, rhythm and beat. Concepts such as fast/slow, heavy/light, loud/soft were extended through movement to music. She also used visual prompts more, for example, making cards for a songboard (Figure 4.2) so that children could make choices

Figure 4.2 A songboard provides visual and linguistic cues that closely connect with gestural and aural communication modes.

and work out which song to expect next. She also set up a visual activity board to assist children to participate in a range of experiences and develop some 'planning and time utilization skills.'

Cindy was very clear about the educational outcomes she was pursuing with her class. She wanted to:

- provide children with the opportunity to engage in meaningful experiences
- enable them to learn at their own pace
- develop confidence and a willingness to participate in new experiences in a range of modalities
- develop individual creativity and imagination based on their interests
- initiate and communicate ideas and feelings
- engage in social interactions with others while developing language and turn-taking skills.

These educational intentions then guided the multiliteracies and ICT choices she made, what she noticed and valued in children's responses and her general enthusiasm.

Our project enables us to stay with Alex as a research participant in his transition to school. The next section explores how he responded to a different pedagogical style and approach to literacy learning in his Year 1 classroom.

Alex in his first year at primary school

Eva and Julia share a multi-age class of preschool and Year 1–2 children. When they first met Alex on a visit they made to his preschool, he presented as a confident, articulate and happy child. Since starting primary school, he is generally always very alert to what is going on around him and what others are doing. However, in their reflections on Alex as a learner, Eva and Julia felt that this alertness has 'taken a while to carry over into his learning'.

Initially, Alex's oral language and confidence led Eva and Julia to have high expectations of his print literacy. Soon, however, they were concerned about his engagement in a range of inappropriate behaviours and eventually attributed this to his lack of understanding. Eva thought that Alex was 'a lower functioning' child who knew what he was writing but was hard to engage. She thought he showed signs of autism and observed he was not enthusiastic about using pencil and paper, although he liked to sharpen pencils and hide bits.

From an early stage in the year, Alex was able to identify each child's locker in the room and loved giving out the take-home books at the end of the day. He was able to recognize all the children's names and also knew every child's lunchbox and drink bottle.

Despite his competence with these things, Eva expressed concern regarding Alex's social skills:

> He loses equipment from the classroom and gets an obsession about things. He loves the computer but it's not productive. He just plays games. Sometimes he gets to go on and do Galaxy Maths – but he just clicks and opens up different things. In play Alex often withdraws himself and sits away from the group.

Alex as an early literacy learner

Eva reported that Alex found it very difficult, both at school and at home, to engage with print. His mother also found it difficult to get him to sit down and look at his take-home books. Alex's teachers perceived that he was a competent oral language user but was a reluctant writer during his first 6 months at school. He tended to copy others' work and look for models. He loved helping others and Eva tried to catch him doing the right thing so that he was not hearing constant corrections. His best writing samples had been obtained in a focused reading group – it was possible to make out 'I see smoke'. Eva had prompted him to think of a sentence that had 'see' in it. By mid-year she had found that he would only write in a focused writing group but seemed to be hearing the ends of words.

Alex initially took no interest in the take-home list of words. Children were asked to choose some and practise writing them. By mid-year he was a little bit keener because other children had moved on to the 100 most frequently used words. Eva did not think Alex seemed particularly interested in words. She initially had him in a higher reading group at the start of the year but had lowered him in mid-year because 'others were zooming past him'.

Alex's interests included the film *Finding Nemo*. He was asked by his teacher to represent aspects of the story setting on a Y chart (which is a graphic organizer requiring brainstorming around three dimensions: what a topic/setting 'looks like', 'feels like' and 'sounds like'; see Figure 4.3). On completion of this task Eva was concerned that:

> Alex had drawn pictures but was on the wrong task. He drew what he could see but not the setting. He'd drawn the characters which wasn't what we wanted.

Eva was concerned that the chart was supposed to be about the setting and that Alex:

> had a lot of trouble explaining – we wanted him to describe the setting, he said it was dark and squishy. He doesn't have the setting in his head.

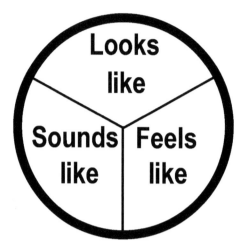

Figure 4.3 Example of a Y chart.

Her assessment of Alex's response as 'incorrect' may have been viewed differently if a multimodal perspective had been considered. His confused response may have indicated that Alex had a poor understanding of the task. Given his abilities on other tasks, it is possible that he may have been able to represent the setting for the movie using a visual mode first, to draw the setting. This may have enabled the print to arise from the visual representation of the setting.

Snapshot of Alex in the primary classroom

Eva's class has a strong focus on beginning literacy. During an observation, Alex was sitting in his classroom at a table, writing. When approached, he announced 'I cheating'. He indicated a sheet taped to his table with 20 words on it. 'Looks like I didn't write that one', he said, indicating a word on the list and proceeding to copy it. 'Eva likes when I do all this writing.' When asked about writing sentences he responded, 'I don't really do sentences' despite having three sentences at the start of his list – 'I see Mum, I see Dad, I see Allison.' He was not convinced when they were pointed out to him! He continued copying words, saying 'Eva will be really proud of me!' When encouraged to sequence a few other words into a sentence he did not seem to be enthusiastic, and announced 'That's enough!' as he went over to give his book to Eva before sitting on the floor.

During the session, Eva called Alex up to share his work. First she asked him, 'Where are the sentences?' Alex replied, 'I didn't write sentences. Eva looked at his page and said, 'Yes you did' – and pointed to them (e.g. 'I see Mum'). Alex then attempted to read out the words he had written. He knew most of them but floundered on several, including 'the'. As a support strategy, Eva asked the class, 'Who can help?' as well as writing 'the' on the board. One of the class read the word and then she encouraged Alex to keep writing sentences.

At Eva's request, the class then moved into pre-organized rotating group activities. Group 1 were set a crossword. Eva prepared the children to be successful by reading out each clue and asking the group for suggestions. Alex knew the answer to the clue 'What is half fish and half girl?' Group 2 were given a Yes/No sheet about sea stars. Again Eva made sure the group knew what was expected of them and went through each statement with them. Alex knew some of the answers. Group 3 were decorating a sea star, while Group 5 were practising writing the letter 'z' in their handwriting book.

Group 4 (Alex's group) were using the computer. Eva had purchased a 'Finding Nemo' program as she knew this was an interest of Alex's. He began by saying 'I think I'll choose Dory.' This was a memory game, similar to turning over cards, where he had to match the fishes. After three or four tries without 100% success he said, 'I don't want to play this.'

The next game was a puzzle game. He showed very good persistence with this, despite lining up one piece correctly about five times and it refused to stick, but finally announced, 'I don't want to play this.' He returned to Dory, saying 'Who cares' and continued trying to match the fishes. He scouted around a couple of other games but wasn't sure what to do with them.

This software, like many others of its kind, does not afford opportunities for open-ended responses, with right or wrong answers and no gradual approximations available to children. They either succeeded or failed based on getting all the answers right in a short space of time. Even though Alex did improve in the number of pairs he achieved each try, there was no record or score of this. If he did not get all correct, he would fail and have to start again. This contrasts sharply with Alex's experience with the open-ended, creative software he had used in preschool, described above.

Introducing new multiliteracies activities in the primary school

When, through their involvement in a collective inquiry process in this research, Eva and Julia read Alex's preschool learning story, their initial reaction was 'It sounds like a different child!' They were startled to realize how different their perceptions of Alex were. Consequently, they had cause to rethink their pedagogies and were mindful of incorporating multimodality in the experiences they provided to the class. They developed a sequence of short lessons that were inspired by Alex's preschool teacher's learning story and his apparent interest in music.

These sessions differed from the general literacy session, in that they were faster-paced, actively engaged children and used a range of communication modes. They were also more specifically tailored to the needs of the small group of children. Julia taught the sessions and joined in with the activities, taking turns with the children.

Julia read a familiar book with a musical theme aloud to the group, stopping at various times during the story to elicit children's responses to parts of the story. They recalled together their favourite parts and Julia encouraged them often, eliciting such responses from Alex as: 'Of course I'm clever! I like that story.' Julia's verbal interaction with the children went beyond mere question and answer, and she was noticeably more conversational in her approach. She shared her opinions and extra information that built upon what the children offered. She also used multiple cues (visual, aural, concrete objects) that children could associate with the printed word, including a printed list of words from the story and pictures of instruments on a chart. After drawing the children's attention to the initial letters of the instrument names on the list and helping children to connect the object's picture with its written name, Julia joined the children in a game using memory cards. Gradually removing these cues, Alex was able to successfully read the printed word in the memory game without any additional cues. Julia also had instruments placed around the classroom, providing another cue for children to make connections between the printed word, the familiar story and the sound the instrument made. In this game Alex experienced frequent success in reading, with children being given the incentive that if they could read the instrument name, they could go and play it. The high energy and sense of fun about the tasks seemed to encourage more risk taking and willingness to 'have a go' by the children. They were highly engaged and keen to persist with the activities.

The way these tasks were structured, with short turn taking and a game-like format, maximized the children's involvement, and such activities seemed to work for Alex in particular. They also helped to maintain Alex's attention. He obviously felt successful, making several comments about being clever. The fact that Julia had gradually removed the stimulus from the aural, visual, print and three-dimensional (concrete) object, to associate only the printed word with the instrument, enabled Alex to succeed in reading the word and his confidence grew. Her knowledge of multimodality had opened up new possibilities for his learning.

Eva also decided to provide Alex with more opportunities to use visual cues. The topic for the term was 'Tools'. She read a big book, *A Check-up with the Doctor*, to the class, then discussed and made a chart about the different tools a doctor used. Alex's literacy rotation that day involved using clip art to insert pictures of tools that a doctor uses and also to use word art to make the matching headings. Alex was able to successfully complete this task independently and also mentored other children to complete the task.

Alex's teachers were able to identify a number of key conditions that they believed helped him to move along a more successful literacy pathway:

- The small group – Alex was not intimidated and felt more confident to answer questions in such an environment. There was also no pressure for Alex to answer all the questions as there would be in a one-to-one situation.
- The use of visual aids along with the text – Alex was able to be successful because he had the visual aids to help him.
- Enjoyable activities – the children responded very well when they thought tasks were enjoyable.
- Alex loves music so was engaged and interested in the tasks that included this.
- Alex achieved success early in the task, which boosted his confidence and he was therefore more willing to take risks in his learning.
- A new environment – conducting the activity outside the regular classroom appeared to provide Alex with an opportunity to reconstruct what the learning environment is about, freeing his preconceptions as to how he thought he should respond.

Alex was much happier when he was given freedom to do independent writing. Self-esteem is really important in this context. In another scenario, Julia gave Alex a camera to take photos whenever he wanted to. He was to write something interesting about the photos as well. This gave him a context and purpose for his writing, and naturally he enjoyed and completed the task successfully.

Commentary

The image of Alex that can be constructed from this is of an alert child, interested in what is going on around him and willing to attend to and pursue particular activities that capture his attention. His teachers have noticed that his interests and the things he chooses to focus on can be unexpected, and one of their challenges is to tap into his interests and build their literacy interventions accordingly.

Like many young children, Alex tended to exhibit restless behaviour in more formal, structured literacy sessions, and his attention to the task or discussion at hand could wander. His primary teachers were conscious of trying not to focus on his sometimes inappropriate behaviour, but at the same time identified that it prevented him from focusing, engaging and learning in the classroom. Similarly, when presented with a writing activity as part of the regular literacy session, Alex had decided that his goal was to produce as many correctly spelt words as he could, despite encouragement by Eva, his class teacher, to use his own words in sentences and read them back for meaning.

One way to understand what might be happening with Alex is that he is experiencing difficulty reading the culture of the literacy session in school, but he has picked up some cues as to what is important (e.g. that words have a particular pattern of spelling), and missed others (e.g. that it is more important to read and write for meaning than to have exact spelling). He also seems to sometimes understand partial cues from his teacher (e.g. his drawings would sometimes represent a different aspect of a story to what the class were focusing on). Moving him to a different environment, such as the hall outside the classroom, seemed to break his preconceptions of what was required so that he was more willing to take risks and make meaningful approximations. The faster pace of a small-group, teacher-led activity with multiple communication cues also seemed to suit his learning style. This raises the question of how important the ability to read the culture of regular literacy sessions is in relation to children's likelihood of experiencing success, and consequently whether some cultures are more likely to foster feelings of self-efficacy and success. Alex's experience contrasts sharply with that of children who were high achievers in the literacy classroom, and they clearly demonstrated that they had worked out what skills and aptitudes had cultural capital, were confident in their ability to apply themselves to such skills and aptitudes, and consequently were confident risk takers whose print literacy practice had developed at a rapid rate.

It is clear that Alex was more engaged when both his interests and preferred ways of learning were identified and used to design experiences for him. They also deepened his capacity to connect different modalities for communicating his ideas to others. Working with Alex using a multiliteracies approach focused on problem solving. It enabled the teachers to think about his lack of success not in terms of what he could not do, but of what new pedagogies they could employ to encourage him to print literacy, recognizing that traditional pathways were not working.

Alex's story prompts reflections on how multiliteracies approaches can enable a more positive image of the child to be constructed, which in turn leads to the development of children's feelings of self-efficacy and subsequently to their successful learning. In particular, the following questions arise:

- How do we construct a primary school curriculum that balances the development of foundational literacy skills with the fostering of children's ideas, interests and curiosity?
- How can foundational print literacy skills be taught in a way that fosters children's sense of self-efficacy and confidence in multiple modes?
- What role might a multiliteracies approach play in such development?
- What is the role of class culture in relation to children's literacy learning?

In relation to Alex, his primary teachers discovered that they could construct more positive learning experiences for Alex by thinking in terms of a pedagogy of multiliteracies. Far from detracting from his learning of print literacy, he clearly gained in confidence in taking risks to read words and he became less concerned with making errors. The use of multiple communication cues for meaning and a gradual withdrawal back to print certainly assisted his ability to decipher print meaningfully. In terms of future directions, the design of multiliteracies activities that were more open-ended could result in the construction of a more positive image of Alex as he clearly possesses a vivid imagination and makes novel connections between ideas. Also using what he can do and is interested in, as a basis for his learning activities, is likely to lead to him becoming a more confident learner.

The notion of how children 'read' the culture of their school or classroom in their first year is also worth considering further. Alex's primary teachers noted that there was considerable pressure from home for Alex to spell correctly, and this may have affected his decisions as to what was most important to concentrate upon in relation to his writing. Alex was identified, by both his preschool teacher and primary teachers, as experiencing some learning difficulties. Making social connections with other children was a challenge for him, which in turn may also have affected his feelings of self-efficacy. Skills such as learning to remember and making plans to complete a task were a challenge for him and may have caused him to disengage at times. Thus, remembering to consider literacy learning in the context of a more holistic view of the child and their learning remains paramount for effective teaching and learning.

Cameron: from problem to promising

Cameron is an Indigenous boy who lives in a metropolitan suburb with his brothers and other extended family including his aunt, who is his legal guardian. His father is in jail and his mother is estranged from the family. Cameron visits his father regularly and sees his mother only occasionally. At the school, 15% of students attending are also Indigenous, including Cameron's older brother.

Cameron in pre-primary

During the middle of the school year, Cameron's preschool teacher, Lucy, became concerned about his speech and receptive language development, and she wondered if this was because Cameron, like many other Indigenous children, might have some hearing loss due to otitis media. His aunt described him as having attention deficit hyperactivity disorder, although his teacher did not observe any school behaviours that would support this. He did not, however, show any interest in listening to stories 'on the mat' and he was described by his teacher as happiest if he was colouring or drawing or playing on the computer, but when he was actually involved in some sort of task requiring language or was asked to give some input in discussion, his usual response was 'I dunno.'

Lucy noted Cameron's strengths in spatial tasks such as block construction, and visual tasks including drawing and painting and using the computer. His artwork was creative and advanced (see Figure 4.4). Cameron's apparent lack of success with routine literacy tasks that were an integral part of schooling was identified and documented, however, at the conclusion of his preschool year. Lucy was worried and at a loss to explain why Cameron had not made progress in the acquisition of alphabetic literacy.

Figure 4.4 Cameron's artwork.

Lucy's prediction for Cameron in the future year at school

Lucy expressed concern for Cameron's alphabetic literacy acquisition and lamented that he had not learned his 'letters' or really demonstrated mastery of 'any sort of English'. She had hoped that on entering Year 1 he would be already demonstrating early or pre-reading skills and she was concerned about how this might affect his participation and sense of self-efficacy in a more formal literacy environment. She noted, in particular, that he would struggle with the more formal Year 1 setting where play was not part of the routine program. She advised that:

> The computer and making it all relate around his interests and family were the ways we captured his attention and helped him retain information.

Whilst Lucy understood where Cameron's strengths lay and what the dimensions of cultural and linguistic diversity were that contributed to his preferred modes of literacy acquisition, she struggled to identify areas within her own pedagogy that might have enabled him to learn the traditional foundational aspects of literacy.

Cameron in his first year of school

In developing a longitudinal picture of Cameron, during his first term in Year 1, we asked the Year 1 teacher to describe Cameron as a literacy learner. Cameron's teacher, Georgie, initially described Cameron this way:

> As a literacy learner, Cameron has difficulty concentrating for long periods . . . has difficulty understanding instructions, is a visual learner, likes to draw and demonstrates talent in this area, can be destructive, draws on tables, carpet or reading books, does not contribute to class discussions, usually takes pride in his work, handwriting is legible and well-presented . . . needs continual support to succeed, makes noises to distract the class, displays some attention-seeking behaviours, is compliant and accepts consequences of his behaviour . . . he cannot differentiate sounds or make connections between symbols and sounds . . . he likes to be read to and will choose to 'read' a book at silent reading time, as this is usually a picture flick he becomes easily bored and will try to wander around the room. He likes to play and finds the formal situations hard to cope with. He is not writing on his own yet but can draw his news and tell the teacher what to scribe. He tends to pick familiar story lines and does not willingly take risks in language.

Georgie also noted that Cameron's rate of learning was below what she would have expected for his age, saying that

> he takes a long time to learn new concepts, he is a kid that you have to go over and over again and generally in a one-to-one situation.

Clearly, in a class of 25 students, it is not always possible for the teacher to provide the opportunities necessary to meet Cameron's learning needs. As the year progressed, Cameron slipped further and further behind his peers. Formal testing by a school psychologist identified Cameron as a 'student at educational risk' and he was placed in a special intervention programme in Term 1. This programme was designed to improve his early literacy skills in a small-group situation. However, although he was able to tell and draw number stories for the teacher to transcribe, in Term 3 he was deemed by the teacher to be making 'limited progress' in print literacy.

However, Georgie did notice that Cameron took great pride in his work when he felt competent and valued as a learner. When it came to print time (handwriting lessons), Georgie observed his behaviour change. It seemed he enjoyed the work, and this was, according to her, because he was 'good' at it. She said:

> He can do beautiful printing and it is very legible and well presented and he'll say, 'What do you think of that Miss?' and I'll say 'Well I think that's fantastic' and he'll just beam. So all that fine motor skill stuff he's really quite good at.

She also told of an instance where the class was engaged in a graphing exercise using little packets of sweets containing a variety of colours, and the children were asked to count and tally them and then to put them on a graph. Cameron did this quickly and accurately, he was the first student to finish and the teacher admitted that her first response to his speed and accuracy was that he must have copied the child sitting next to him. She checked and noticed that his neighbour had completely different data and that Cameron had, in fact, generated this completely independently. Georgie stated that she was shocked by this unanticipated competence and noted that this was linked to and confirmed her previous observations of Cameron's strengths in the visual/spatial area:

> I could see he was giving me many clues about the way he learnt and how he made meaning in a visual mode. I realized that if I worked in the visual/spatial areas I could be using his strengths to reach his linguistic literacy ... he already knew things about literacy I was busily teaching to others.

When Cameron's pre-primary teacher visited him in the Year 1 class, she noted:

> He was always asked to sit at the front so he was not distracting others . . . he got his book and started working, he was on task and looking at his page of work (word sleuth) while a lot of other children were talking he was sitting quietly . . . at times Cameron asked Georgie for help and was able to wait for help until the teacher was able to give it to him . . . basically he completed the task independently . . . this behaviour was interesting as this was not how he behaved in pre-primary, we found it difficult to keep him interested and on task a lot of the time.

Multiliteracies and pedagogical change

As described in Chapter 3, the collective inquiry approach to our research project entailed the inclusion of successive teachers across the life of the study. Wherever possible, each focus child had at least two of their successive early childhood teachers engaged in the research. This longitudinal approach to change and in-depth inquiry was one factor that we felt ensure the successes of the project. Teachers reported their immense professional satisfaction derived from opportunities to engage in ongoing conversations with colleagues who had taught or were currently teaching a child whom they had taught. Their discussions provided opportunities to reflect, critique, evaluate and gain insight over time. When Georgie entered the research circle at the end of Term 1, she expressed frustration with her programme for Cameron and was bewildered that her entire repertoire of (alphabetic) literacy strategies was not reaching him as a literacy learner. She was motivated to try something new.

After the introductory research circle, in which we explored multimodality, Georgie recorded in her journal:

> the penny dropped – Cameron was indeed literate but expressing his understanding in a different mode. I realised that if I worked in the visual and spatial modes I could be using his strengths to reach his linguistic literacy.

And so Georgie set about devising experiences to engage Cameron. She decided to introduce the digital camera to him as a tool for storytelling.

Creating narrative with digital photography

The day following the teacher research circle, Georgie invited Cameron to create a 'camera story'. He asked if that was like a movie. Once he was shown the basic functions of the camera, Cameron proceeded as follows:

- He selected props to tell his story.
- He decided he wanted to make his friend Charlie the main character.
- With assistance from the teacher he developed a storyline based on the props he had chosen.
- He gave prolonged attention to this task.
- He checked camera angles through the lens before capturing shots.
- He asked numerous questions and listened intently to explanations about how the computer could take images from the camera.
- At the end of the session he was keen to show the other children his digital story and to explain how he did it.
- He showed pride in his work and was aware that Charlie and the other children were impressed. This was a cue for Cameron to understand that his work was valued.

Cameron was able, at that moment, to demonstrate the complexity of thinking he was capable of, including his attention to detail and accuracy which he clearly valued as important elements of the task. He was curious, challenged and engaged. This was the first time in the entire year to date that Georgie had observed Cameron taking an enthusiastic approach to a classroom task.

The story shown in Figure 4.5, developed by Cameron, illustrates his competence in narrative and the ways in which he was able to draw on his 'lifeworld' to generate a multimodal text.

Commentary

Cameron's story gives insight into some critical questions facing educators as they attempt to understand and cater for children from diverse cultural and linguistic backgrounds. For example:

- What do I know about the lives and experiences of the children I teach? What do I need to find out?
- How will I find out?
- What are the children's competencies and interests?
- What can a child's family and community tell me about who they are and how they learn?
- What do families believe is important for their children to learn?
- How can I ensure that there are opportunities for multimodal learning in my programme?

The multimodal capacities that children like Cameron already process on entry to school settings are key entry points for teachers who want to design effective experiences for young children. They provide ways to reach other modes, in order to build an increasing repertoire of multimodality,

Cameron's Story

Charlie had a friend. His name was Calvin.

They had a talk.

Charlie had a boat.

They all went for a ride in the car.

They went to see Calvin's dad at work. He dug holes.

They all went for a day out in the boat.

Figure 4.5 Cameron's story.

enabling children to become multiliterate. These entry points require, as Georgie discovered, a willingness to rethink pedagogy and views of learning, in order to provide a pathway that leads to linguistic and alphabetic learning.

Magic, movement and music: Argyle primary school class

Programme overview

Argyle is a diverse and multicultural school located in the western suburbs of Melbourne. The target class was a multi-age class of preschool and Year 1–2 children and involved both the class teacher and early years literacy co-ordinator. The assistant principal coordinated the programme, with the literacy coordinator taking responsibility for identifying links between the target class programme and other early years classes and programmes. The two creative practitioners working with this school were a dancer/ choreographer and an opera singer/actor.

The central organizing idea for the Argyle programme was around the theme of 'Values', which was arrived at through discussions between the class teacher and coordinating practitioner. This later developed into the idea of a magical bird bringing messages that encapsulated these values, which were communicated in creative ways and through the ideas of the children. Prior to this, children were taught a range of exercises, games and concepts designed to enhance their body confidence, ability to communicate and work together and express their emotions and ideas.

The Argyle team were interested in how students communicate and express their emotions through a variety of different modes (e.g. dance, drama, visual arts) and had a strong grounding in Reggio Emilia philosophy, including the *Hundred Languages of Children* (Malaguzzi 1994) and multiliteracies (Cope and Kalantzis 2000). As the school draws from a community that includes many recent migrants and families from lower socio-economic backgrounds, teachers were keen to find ways that uncovered children's different strengths. Contributions were highly valued, particularly as traditional measures of literacy generally rank many of these children below expected levels. The school has clearly articulated values such as cooperation, respect, acceptance and tolerance and identified self-esteem, empowerment, resilience, communication and empathy as areas to focus on through the action research process.

Practically, the programme began with a focus on developing trust and relationships and introducing children to a range of exercises that became building blocks for later work towards a public performance. Early aims of the programme included:

- development of body awareness and self-expression through movement

- experimenting with and experiencing movement
- introduction of dance skills
- development of a movement vocabulary
- development of ability to reflect on observations and emotions.

The development of confidence and the ability to 'read' visual, gestural and spatial forms of communication were observed very early on in the programme, with children demonstrating both creativity and 'real understanding' in their responses. What was striking about the dance programme was that it was also a communication programme, an area of very high importance in this population of students and not automatically associated with dance. For example 'movement conversations' required students to:

- read the body
- respond to each other
- be a good 'listener'
- be polite – move or 'talk' one at a time
- give somebody your full attention
- respond with body awareness
- be aware of all the other people in the space.

Students learned that communication through body language and voice tone are just as important as words, so these exercises cued students into an extremely important aspect of communication that is often not taught explicitly. Consequently, the children became more skilled in their ability to both understand and initiate more complex forms of communication, a building block of any literate practice.

The programme emphasized the development of foundational skills that were specific to each discipline. For example, in the dance programme the following areas were explicitly taught:

- travelling through space
- moving at different levels
- making shapes and patterns
- new concepts such as improvisation, counterbalance, levels, leaping, whirling, twirling.

The dance practitioner described her process as follows:

> Freedom within interesting structures is . . . opening doors to many of these children . . . I think J [teacher] and I are making connections for the children but it is within these that the children are exploring very creatively and beginning to lead us and create new inspirations for

both of us . . . Within all of this work I was also aiming to highlight the importance of respecting and being aware of your partner and the whole group – linking to the topic of 'Values' being explored in the classroom.

(Teacher reflective journal)

The dance practitioner drew a diagram of her creative practice that illustrates the connections and emphases she makes (see Figure 4.6).

The practice of the opera singer/actor could also be outlined through several stages. She began by establishing the conditions for learning, which included valuing children's knowledge. This was coupled with early activity to build up children's skills and concepts such as linguistics, rhythm and pitch (including whether sounds were high, low, long or short). Students were then encouraged to take small risks in the group and engage in discussion, performance, demonstration and having a go at new ideas. Later this was blended with children's ideas and the overall general direction of the values theme developed in the dance class to produce an integrated performance. Of particular interest in the singer/actor sessions was the valuing of linguistic and cultural diversity. Her broad repertoire of songs in many languages provided children with a strong message about the importance and skill required to speak more than one language. Often children with a first language other than English tend to focus on their proficiency in this dominant language and find themselves struggling to express ideas and understandings. The valuing of multiple languages was another way that multiliterate practices were developed through the programme.

Figure 4.6 Connections in creative practice.

Building trust

The issue of building trust seemed to be much easier with this group of young children as they saw many of the early skill development activities as games, and even those reluctant to participate in the first few weeks soon overcame this and voluntarily joined in with the group. The creative practitioner's view was that the role, presence and attitude of the teacher were all crucial to such a positive influence. The class teacher in this case operated in a variety of roles, sometimes participating, observing, and taking notes or photographs. The children were very aware of her at all times and she was always involved, intervening, leading and supporting instinctively in a way that worked for the partnership. The dance practitioner felt that the teacher placed a great deal of trust in her, noting:

> J is really involved in the journey and her interest in individuals and the group is truly focused on the process – she does not make me feel that I have to produce anything at this point – this is unusual as in my experience I have generally found teachers will not trust my process until they see some form of product. We have actually developed a lot of work that will be formalized into a performance piece. J is very trusting of me and also of the children. She has shown she really is prepared to take *risks*!
>
> (CP journal).

The opera singer/actor also had a similar experience, noting that the younger children were much more receptive to her process than the older primary school children she was working with at another school. The children saw the practitioners as safe and interesting adults they could play games with and have fun.

Organizational structures

The programme at Argyle was conducted on a half day each week between 9 a.m. and 1 p.m. This settled into a pattern of whole-class participation before recess and then splitting into two half-class groups after recess. The dance practitioner in particular found this structure better than that whole class together, with groups of 12 being an ideal way to keep the whole class engaged. The singer practitioner did not find whole-class groupings problematic. Space was always a problem, with much of the programme being conducted in a hall between classrooms. Sometimes the school multipurpose room was available. The school, despite its space restrictions, was very prepared to be flexible and work out solutions as best they could with the creative practitioners.

Student outcomes

Even from the first week, teachers and practitioners noted the development of confidence and the ability of children to engage and watch each other. They were able to respond with positive dialogue and articulate what they had learnt, as well as discuss feelings. By week 3 of the programme children were taking greater risks in trying new ways of work, building stories and ideas as well as articulating and representing feelings. The creative practitioner wrote:

> The growing confidence is allowing and enabling them to explore and experience movement in new ways. I particular noticed three boys who made great breakthroughs in this work – all three have been previously been quite shy and lacking in confidence and until this week had not seemed to be fully engaged in the workshops ... The responses were very creative and way beyond my expectations ... The children embrace each idea with enthusiasm but also really think about what I am asking them to do or discover.
>
> (CP journal)

In addition, the teachers documented a whole range of other positive benefits and gains as a result of participating in the programme. These included:

- children remembering concepts and including them in their impro-visations
- increased articulation and demonstration of imagination
- sustained dancing and focus for whole sessions
- creative and unusual ideas and responses
- development of confidence and courage
- enthusiasm and focus
- ability to follow and link formal directions with creative tasks
- shy children taking on leadership roles successfully
- children relying on each other and committing to the process
- children articulating how much they love dancing and singing – passion for what they are doing
- skill development and persistence to excel through rehearsals
- integration of skills into other work
- inventiveness
- self-regulation and rigour
- development of empathy.

> In one of our pieces, the students have had to devise a short move-ment piece in groups of 3 or 4. They have applied themselves and developed a beginning, middle and finish ... They are beginning to

show independence and an ability to solve problems and perform a group task using movement. This is an amazing outcome for such young children. Again we are noting how all children in the group have moments where they excel way beyond our expectations … some are really extending themselves as they try to find and experience new ways of moving. They are taking risks and finding new success.

(CP journal)

The opportunity to learn through dance and singing has provided some children with alternative pathways to learning that are more in line with their individual learning preferences. The programme has provided them with strong messages that what they are comfortable with and good at is valued (as opposed to the image they often develop of themselves as struggling literacy learners). It has also provided them with space to show what they know and to express themselves in a safe environment. For some children, this programme has been their first experience of success at school and the ensuing confidence has led to them taking greater risks in their classroom print literacy experiences. For example, one girl who was reluctant to write began enthusiastically drawing and writing after dance class. The programme has changed some children's motivation to attend school. Another girl who was only attending school one or two days per week loved and excelled at dance to such a degree that she put pressure on her mother to get her to school on dance days and this has gradually increased her general attendance over the year. Her delight in her own capacity was obvious to observe and there was no need for anyone to tell her that she was highly skilled and talented when dancing. Children were able to articulate the following in relation to the programme:

I feel best when I rehearse. I do my best when I perform in front of my parents.

I felt really good when I performed. I didn't feel shy at all.

Learning how to dance made me very happy.

Some kids tried to be brave.

It was hard to learn about how to be good to people.

When I sing it's hard to be loud enough, and I shake because I am shy.

Young children generally appear to connect the notion of creativity with art and were able to articulate aspects of the ideas exchange process:

Let it out.

Write it/draw it.

Don't rush it.

Make a story out of it.

Children reported a range of different kinds of learning as a result of working with a creative practitioner. They thought it helped them to learn how to work in groups, express their opinions and speak up and to trust each other more. Some reported that it helped with their English and gave them new skills. Children learnt that it was 'OK to be different' and the creative practitioners 'tried to help us be better at things we had never done before'. They felt 'more responsible for what we do' and believed the programme helped them to express their opinions and 'speak up'.

Star Wars project [1]

Background

The Year 1 classroom in which the following scenario took place is located at Bridgewater Central School, an independent coeducational school. The school's philosophy and approach were inspired by the Reggio Emilia schools in Italy. In the class there are 24 students aged 5–7 years and two qualified teachers, Amy and Reece. Both teachers aspire to implement social constructivism principles to support student learning and promote *The Hundred Languages of Children* (Malaguzzi 1994).

Bridgewater CS directs a large portion of its budget to acquiring a diverse range of ICT resources and the employment of a full-time staff member for ICT support. Also facilitating ICT integration in student learning are weekly visits to Tesori, a community reusable materials resource centre. At the centre, students explore items and experiment with imagery using ICT in the centre's Light and Shadow room.

The Children's Star Wars Project evolved through emergent curriculum and was driven by student interests (Dewey 1899). At Bridgewater CS, children's projects can extend over long periods of time – weeks, months, and in the case of the Children's Star Wars Project, for the entire school year. ICT is used in various forms throughout the project. Most significantly, ICT is used for creative design purposes and remains largely in the hands of the child. The description that follows is based on fieldwork observations and interviews with Reece, and provides insight to these processes.

---

[1] This project was documented by Sandra Hesterman, School of Education, Murdoch University, Western Australia.

Star Wars popular culture

In the summer of 2005, media hype surrounding the premiere of the last *Star Wars* movie, *Return of the Sith*, was at its most frenzied. It came as no surprise when, at the commencement of the new school year, there were students in Reece's class enthusiastic to initiate a *Star Wars* project.

In early February the *Star Wars* project group was formed. Reece informed us:

> The New Star Wars movie sequel, advertising, toys and video games motivated children to participate in anything to do with Star Wars.

During their first project meeting, a group of five interested boys met to discuss *Star Wars*. They wanted to design a new movie sequel, to become characters in a *Star Wars* story.

Star Wars design

Reece videotaped the action when the children were spontaneously role playing with paper light sabres (Figure 4.7). Later, the recording was viewed by the class. Other students said: 'We don't actually get what's happening! They're just running and playing and doing sword fighting.' The Star Warians met to critically reflect on peer feedback and consider how to improve story detail. Reece describes this process in an interview:

> After discussing their ideas with one another, the group discussed components of their story. Some children just wanted to start the story with a fight with Luke Skywalker being the winner – the end. However, one boy was very vocal and commented, 'You need him to go exploring, find a planet with baddies, then a fight. He wins and then flies home.' After discussing how stories are developed, that is beginning–middle–end, the children agreed the boy's story 'sounded right'. Therefore, it was decided that this would form the basis of their story script.

As a result of this meeting, they identified two main story events: an exploratory galactic spaceship flight; and a light sabre battle between 'goodies' and 'baddies' where good triumphs over evil.

Over time, the boys' shared interest in a *Star Wars* story extends to wanting to make a movie. They aim to duplicate authentic *Star Wars* culture in their movie, its characters, language, costumes, and music and space adventure. Reece provides time, opportunity and resources for students to explore ideas,

Figure 4.7 Light sabre role play.

experiment with design features and collaborate in democratic decision making (Dewey 1899).

Early-stage design work

A popular project activity is designing spaceship models (Figure 4.8). The boys access an assortment of classroom resources, and although the designs appear simplistic the language used by members to describe features provides insight into their extensive understandings of spaceships. They take digital photographs of their spaceships and Reece labels their features. The boys also consider how they can improvise flight in their movie. ICT is used to design scenery backdrops, space ships and planets. To further stimulate interest in this activity, Reece accesses NASA's images of planets and moons in the solar system via the Internet and projects these on to classroom walls. Students share their

Figure 4.8   Student designs for spaceships.

knowledge about space and study non-fiction books on the science of planet hunting, identification and exploration. Other books examined include popular culture magazines, comics, visual dictionaries and *Star Wars* storybooks.

During the weekly visit to Tesori, students select materials to design props and create costume accessories to make their *Star Wars* film look and feel like the 'real thing'. On the day of the recording, the boys change into costumes, position masks, take hold of light sabres, and await Reece's direction. Two of the students took charge of the recording, the rest of the group seemed to have a strong sense of the script they had jointly written and commenced acting out the story. Some issues became immediately apparent: there was insufficient light and stage direction was poor, and some members were unhappy about their costumes. The first recording of the movie, although a little chaotic, was heralded a success by the group.

Redesign work

The next school day began with a class viewing of the children's *Star Wars* movie. Reece's inclusion of the authentic scrolling of the *Star Wars* introduction was met with approving nods from members of the group. In the final moments of the film luminous shooting stars spread across the screen. The children are enthralled by this unexpected special effect. Where had the stars come from? Whilst editing the video footage Reece decided to introduce the children to the idea of special effects. This decision proves instrumental in presenting a new dimension to students' movie design. Group members' understanding of what is now possible motivates them to redesign their script, desiring a higher level of sophistication.

After the screening of the Take 1 movie, the class participates in a movie review. The following extract from field notes taken by the researcher documents their critical reflection.

> It is no good. It's all wobbly.
>
> You couldn't see Rory at all.
>
> It was dark.
>
> I think we need more light.
>
> We need a real gun noise.
>
> Yeah, we need electric effects.
>
> Hey, we need the Force in our movie.

During an interview, Reece commented on the children's desire for special effects.

> The biggest stepping-stone from the first movie to the second movie was children's need for special effects. Not just the voice-over. They wanted the zapping and shooting sounds. Because I added the special effects, they could see what was possible and said, 'Wow, that's what we want.' So that changed the movie tone from finishing in Term 3 to, well okay we have a whole term before the end of the year to put in the special effects!

In the weeks that followed, group members documented changes to the movie. They folded sheets of A4 paper, drew existing scenes on one side, then, using arrows, identified modifications on the other side of the paper. These suggestions were discussed during project meetings. The group suggested that:

> Instead of fighting, the Millennium Falcon can blow up.
>
> I am going to make music and I am going to colour my light sabre in red.
>
> I am going to share the video camera so I don't get tired.

I want to be in the battle.

Instead of running around and using our light sabres as bullets, we can try to make ships.

At the end of Term 3, Reece requested from Jon (the ICT support staff) assistance to facilitate the use of 'the blue screen' and inclusion of special effects, both visual and aural, in the children's Take 2 movie production. Reece commented:

> The only reason we went down that route was because I had Jon on board. Jon was willing to help. There is no way I could physically manage doing all that editing that Jon did and still get them to act and do all the other things at the same time. It was a huge commitment timewise to do that.

In order to portray *Star Wars* authentically, children brought Star Wars Lego models from home to use as props. Jon facilitated the creation of 'light' and 'dark side' music using GarageBand software. They experimented with different electronic sounds to create special effects. The boys also designed a diorama and attached fishing line to their Lego spaceship models so as suspend them in the diorama space. They engaged in imaginary play, and this provided group members with an opportunity to design new scripts.

A blue tarpaulin sheet was secured on to one of the classroom walls, thus creating the 'blue screen' (see Figure 4.9). Reece assumes the role of director, Jon the producer and Star Warians the actors. Unlike 'Star Wars Movie Take 1', 'Star Wars Movie Take 2' is a staged performance. During the re-enactment of each scene, the boys are reminded of the camera position and asked to adopt a profile or frontal body position so that their gestures are clearly communicated. The audio recording of voice-over ensures they will be heard. Reece demonstrates to the children how they might move their body if they were travelling in a real spaceship. Finally, the recording is complete.

Star Wars celebration

On their first viewing of '*Star Wars* Take 2' everyone is enthralled when they view miniaturized Star Warians sitting in the cockpit of their Lego model spaceship flying across the screen. The culmination of a year's project work is realized and they are truly ecstatic. One child comments:

> Jon shrank us and put us on mini spaceships! He gave us the Force!

Figure 4.9   Experimenting with the blue screen.

Star Wars reflections

Reece's reflections on the Children's Star Wars Project and in particular his role in the process:

> When we first started, it wasn't actually to make a *Star Wars* movie or a DVD. It just ended up going in that direction because that's what the children wanted to do. The movie part came along as the project evolved. The process was open-ended. Very early on in the piece, they wanted to see themselves on the computer or on TV. There's only certain ways to achieve this, some form of video or a DVD or some other electronic means. My aim was to get a storyline with a script. The costumes and everything else was up to them. They were given free range to do whatever they wanted to do.

Summary

The stories in this chapter have demonstrated the ways in which multimodality has been a particular pedagogical focus in four different settings. The first two stories document the learning of two individual children whose teachers provided opportunities for them to learn simultaneously in different modes. The others explain how two different communities of learners utilized multiple modalities to create innovative projects.

Popular culture is a feature of this chapter, with various examples of children's cultural literacy around music, movies, games and the Internet. Students who are comfortable with a hybrid of media dimensions are the generation that now inhabit our classrooms. Children in the earliest years of schooling are more fluent in their use of ICT than any previous generation and are able to 'work interchangeably and simultaneously in multiple modes which are animated, gestural, visual, and written' (Rowsell 2006: 17). As a consequence of this, pedagogies also need to be transformed to take account of the sophisticated skills students bring to school (Yelland 2007). This chapter has drawn on empirical research to demonstrate the ways in which multimodal experiences should be included as an integral part of school activities in order to bridge the gap between traditional literacies and the new multiliteracies that are fundamental to learning in the twenty-first century.

5 Connecting with identities for enhanced learning

Introduction

This chapter begins with a discussion about the personal, social and cultural practices which impact on the lives of children in our classrooms. The discussion draws on postmodernist understandings of childhoods, which challenge traditional developmentalist discourses that universalize childhood and focus on comparing individual children to a set of preconceived 'norms'. In the new discourses, the focus shifts to a consideration of collaborative ways of knowing and learning which includes the co-construction of knowledge and values the strengths and capabilities that are characteristic of the diverse lifeworlds of children. The chapter explores notions of identity and interrogates the ways in which teachers can understand the child as an active learner with reference to specific examples from the empirical data. Issues related to self-image and the ways in which we can use funds of knowledge (Moll *et al.* 1992) and incorporate them into school experiences are considered and linked to cases of the focus children from our project work. The results of the research indicate that teachers can effectively include and extend connections with children's lifeworlds via the pedagogy of multiliteracies and in so doing create a sense of belonging. Such pedagogies can strengthen the self-image and generate positive dispositions for learning for individuals, while simultaneously helping to build interdependent and collaborative learning communities.

Contemporary understandings of childhoods

In recent years some of the prevailing truths of childhood and young children's learning inherent within modernist discourses have been scrutinized and interrogated by postmodernist thinkers and researchers (Cannella 1997; Greishaber and Cannella 2001; James and Prout 1990; MacNaughton 2000). For example, members of the Reconceptualising Early Childhood Group have critiqued the notions of childhood embedded within developmentalist discourses that have characterized the identity of young children in terms of immaturity, inno-cence and vulnerability (Fleer 1995; Kessler and Swadener 1992). Researchers and scholars within this group have recognized the ways in which develop-mentalist pedagogy privileges the practices of the dominant culture while excluding and devaluing the diversity and complexity of experience and knowledge that exists within the lived experience of children within diverse families and community groups (e.g. Cannella 1997; Silin 1995). The edu-cational experience of Reggio Emilia in Italy, where pedagogy is informed by conceptualizations of childhood as a time of curiosity, creativity and cultural participation, has also offered an alternative view.

Children generate many theories and hypotheses for interpreting their surroundings, but these often remain unexpressed because they are not asked for or listened to. We should be aware of how little we actually know about children's autonomous learning strategies and their ideas about the world and themselves from their perspectives and through their explanations. If we asked children and documented their responses respectfully, we would gain greater insights into their curiosity, feelings, views and potential. The process would also raise many questions and issues around what constitutes learning and teaching, and this is viewed as a positive thing that would minimize the likeli-hood of our making overly rapid generalizations about the information that we gather (Castignetti and Vecchi 1997: 94).

A positive view of the child as capable, knowledgeable and autonomous challenges the notion of the adult–child binary and diminishes the traditional hierarchical relationships that exist between adults and children which con-tinue to be pervasive within educational contexts. Traditional approaches frequently silence and disempower children as learners. In new approaches to learning the lived experiences of children are legitimate sites of learning within educational settings.

Contemporary notions of identity

During the period of early childhood (from birth to 8 years of age) young children are increasingly moving into, and between, the familiar contexts of home and family and settings of care and education. Early experiences of care and education provide young children with important opportunities to explore, express and reflect on aspects of their personal, cultural and social experience and to determine who they are in relation to others. As active participants of a social group, young children learn about relationships and in so doing explore the rights and responsibilities that come with being a mem-ber of a particular social group. In the process they gain further understandings about their own capabilities and identities as learners. Transition to school further highlights the significance of identity in the learning process as young children endeavour to read and interpret the expectations of this more formal context (Dockett and Perry 2007).

Contemporary understandings of childhood also challenge traditional notions of identity. Rather than being seen as an unfolding process towards a unified and cohesive essence of self (e.g. Erikson 1968), contemporary views suggest that identity is an abstraction that is hybrid, fluid and contextual. For example, McCarthey and Moje (2002: 231) suggest:

> identity [is] hybrid, . . . constructed from multiple experiences and relationships that are enacted within particular spaces and places. . . . identity can be hybrid, it can be complex, and it can be fluid and shifting as a person moves from space to space and relationship to relationship.

This is reinforced by Sarup (1998) who defined identity as a 'construction, a consequence of interactions between people, institutions and practices' (1998: 11) and suggested that identities are formed within relationships with others, and are constantly subject to the influences of those people and institutions around us and thus full of 'contradictions and ambiguities' (1998: 14).

This view of identity has significant implications for early childhood educational settings and for the pedagogy that is implemented. The lived experiences that children bring to educational contexts reflect contemporary times in which we live in a multimodal world, a globalized economy, where current world issues such as sustainability and climate change are pervasive. Malaguzzi (1994) argued that early education must reflect and be responsive to a broader view of education, which encapsulates a diverse range of experiences:

> Talk about education (including education for young children) cannot be confined to its literature. Such talk, which is also political, must continuously address major social changes and transformations in economy, science, arts and human relationships and customs. All of these larger forces influence how human beings – even young children – read and deal with the realities of life. They determine the emergence on both general and local levels of new methods of educational context and practice, as well as new problems and soul searching questions.

A focus on the pedagogy of multiliteracies in the early years provides a context for the use of ICT in contemporary childhoods and uncovers the power of multimodal learning in the early years that was discussed in the previous chapter. As Haas Dyson (2003) argued, references to media and shared childhood cultures are more than topics that are of interest to children. They are sources of identity and the context for peer connections and relationships.

This also makes them sites of identity construction and representation. During our work with teachers in the research project it became apparent that incorporating a pedagogy of multiliteracies enabled aspects of the personal, social and cultural experiences of young children, which may have been overlooked or seen as deficits within traditional understandings of language and literacy learning, to be reconceptualized as assets. When viewed as assets, personal, social and cultural experiences were identified, discussed and extended and shared with others in ways which transformed learning and teaching for both the adults and the children in their centres or classrooms.

The cases

The cases in this chapter focus on individual learners and their transition from their preschool to the more formal context of school. The cases illustrate the ways in which the pedagogy of multiliteracies enabled teachers to build connections with the personal, social and cultural practices that comprise children's worlds, enabling children to represent and explore aspects of their lived experience in multimodal ways. These connections proved to be powerful in building relationships and enhancing the individual learning potential of young children. The outcomes indicated that through this process children, as active members, were able to strengthen their own positive dispositions towards learning and with their teachers collaboratively create a community of learners.

Background

Jane and Cody, aged 4, were members of the preschool group at a community-based early learning centre located in a culturally diverse area of Sydney with a high level of public housing and socio-economic disadvantage. The centre offers a rich educational programme for children from 6 weeks to 5 years. In the following year Cody and Jane began attending the nearby primary school. They were placed in different classes from the beginning of their first year, which is called kindergarten in this state. Cody was allocated to a kindergarten class while Jane joined a composite kindergarten–Year 1 class. Cody's background is Anglo-Australian, while Jane is Chinese–Australian and bilingual in English and Mandarin.

Pedagogical approaches at the early learning centre

At the commencement of the research project, Jane and Cody, as members of the preschool group at the early learning centre, were active participants in a full-day programme of play and learning experiences within both the indoor and outdoor environments. Play resources at the centre included traditional early childhood resources such as blocks, domestic play props, construction materials, puzzles, books, sand and water, as well as computers with a range of commercial computer programs.

Observations of the centre's daily operations and discussions with teachers revealed that the philosophies and practices of staff reflected contemporary perspectives of childhood. The programme provided was based on an image of the child as strong, resourceful and capable. The play and learning experiences and resources offered to children built on their strengths and interests as well as their lifeworlds (family and community experiences). The teacher's work in literacy was enacted around an understanding of literacy as a social practice. Within the centre, literacy practices evident in the home context were supported with the provision of culturally relevant resources and experiences, such as newspapers in a range of scripts, magazines, recipe books, and cooking experiences. The introduction of the ideas associated around a pedagogy of multiliteracies that incorporated the effective use of ICT built on the existing pedagogical approaches used at the centre and were seen as an extension to the children's literacy learning by the children's teacher, Megan.

Funds of knowledge

Megan was very committed to finding out what funds of knowledge the children brought with them to the centre. This included establishing what skills and access to ICT the children had within their homes and communities. For example, she noted in her reflective journal:

> Find out what they can do at home. Eg using computer, video, tv, cd player etc.

She gathered information about the children's existing skills in terms of being multiliterate and their use of ICT by talking further with them and their families. She offered the children access and exposure to familiar technologies in the programme (e.g. cooking with the microwave) and then incorporated new technologies, including using a digital camera (Figure 5.1), video camera and particular computer programs. Megan encouraged the children to be creative in their explorations and extended their problem-solving skills via effective scaffolding when things did not quite work out as planned. The salience and personal significance of these experiences for the children meant that ICT supported their explorations and learning and enabled them to access information, take risks and reveal previously undisclosed aspects of their identity.

Figure 5.1 Experimenting with the digital camera.

Teaching strategies

Megan used a range of strategies to provide contexts for her children to explore multiliteracies. Her comments reflect some of these approaches:

> I installed Kid Pix and let them explore the program. I tried to be sitting near the computer during the first week so I could answer any questions the children had. I explained the basic tools such as paint-brush and how to change the colour of the brush. I explained that if we saved the pictures we could print them out later. I saved the pictures and explained what I was doing.
>
> After the initial interest in the digital camera we practised using a disposable camera and talked about all the important things we need to remember when taking photos. We worked out some rules together. E.g. You need to – Put your hand in the strap. Hold with both hands. Look in the view-finder. Press the button and hold still and listen to the teacher. This afternoon Jane asked if she could use the digital camera. I showed her how to take a shot and she had a try. She walked around the room with the camera and chose children to take photos of. She asked for help to look at the photos she had taken.

Megan was providing resources and a learning environment that enabled the children to work with images, text, music and other sounds. In introducing new programs on the computer and other new technologies, she facilitated a thoughtful blend of child-initiated explorations and investigations (situated practice), and also included more direct (overt instruction) teaching through demonstration and explanation. This more direct teaching was grounded in the authentic experiences of the children, occurred in small interest groups and was highly responsive to the children's immediate interests, strengths and desire to know more. As Plowman and Stephen (2007) argue in their discussion of 'guided participation', Megan's teaching strategies in relation to ICT were consistent with the child-centred pedagogy of the centre. She was sensitive to the ways in which the children engaged with ICT and was able to work with the focus of their learning in order to identify the optimal point for her intervention.

ICT and multiliteracies: documentation

As is evident in many early childhood settings (e.g. Arthur *et al.* 2005; Fleet *et al.* 2006), the children in the centre were familiar with the use of technology for documenting their play and learning. They had seen the digital camera used by teachers and other adults to capture moments of play and learning and were frequently involved in revisiting and discussing these images and their associated play experiences with other children, teachers and families. Child participation also involved helping to record the accompanying stories for the daily classroom diary, for individual portfolios or for documentation of play and learning for the walls of the centre.

During the research project the children increasingly used the various technologies that teachers used for documentation of learning and for sharing the knowledge that was acquired as a result of specific investigations. The teachers invited the children to increase their participation in the documentation of examples of their own play and work. As their participation increased, the children became more familiar and skilled with both the technology of resources as well as the roles that the new technologies have in recording events (documentation) and also as a regular and important way of communicating and sharing ideas with others. For example, Jane showed her friends her knowledge of Chinese characters by drawing some Chinese characters with the paintbrush tool in Kid Pix. Other children also wanted to share their particular interests in and knowledge of examples of popular culture. This led to them being involved in planning, scripting and videoing various dramatic presentations and scenarios. They took ownership of the creative and planning processes associated with the use of video as a tool of documentation.

The more diverse forms of documentation that emerged reflected the children's lived experiences and their diverse and fluid identities. The computer, video and digital camera enabled sharing of ideas that reflected the interests and identities of the children involved rather than the documentation agenda of the teacher. Megan noted:

> Our use of ICT and commitment to multiliteracies gave us a new window on the child. We could see more of what the children know and understand, the diversity of their skills, learning styles and temperaments. Through the technology children revealed themselves 'more' not 'less'.

ICT and multiliteracies: playful explorations

After a period of experimentation and exploration with various types of ICT, the children embraced the use of the camera and made videos as part of their play. The children demonstrated and explored their knowledge and experience of the genre of television and broader popular culture modes within the context of their imaginative play. They interviewed each other and their teachers and created video clips to show their special skills and talents, such as dancing and singing. This style reflected the current television programmes that the children were familiar with. They also combined ICT with more traditional play resources (e.g. dressing up, painting and collage) to create landscapes and backdrops to support their video narratives. Additionally, they incorporated sound effects from various sources, such as with musical instruments, and from the environment (e.g. city sounds and birds singing).

The subsequent downloading of the footage from the video camera to the computer added to the experience, as children watched and critiqued the results of their explorations. ICT became a valuable part of the play process, extending the possibilities for children by enabling them to include actions, ideas and knowledge from their own lived experiences. This knowledge was used by the children to create real and imaginary scenarios that moved beyond traditional early childhood play resources to include new technologies and techniques, incorporating actions and voices that reflected sophisticated understandings of their contemporary worlds and the artefacts in it.

Megan commented that the digital play space was a popular learning centre in the room. She felt that there was always lots happening there and commented in the following way about one particular piece of video footage:

> K decided she wanted to make a movie of ballerinas so after some discussion with her peers two girls decided to dance for the movie. . . . Cody then decided to interview with the camera. This was his first go with the camera.

Several months later she noted:

> Cody worked independently to make his movie. He wanted to interview one of the staff members . . . the camera ran out of memory so there was only room for one question! Jane and her friend were also very interested in doing interviews. Jane wanted to be interviewed by her friend. Cody later made a movie – 'Cody and the Dinosaur'. Some of the girls wanted to make a music video – this is an early attempt. The boys had an idea to make a movie of their puppet show.

The children's use of ICT as a play artefact became significant with regard to problem solving, self-expression and explorations of identity. The camera, for example, became a medium for storytelling for children whose writing skills would have limited their output significantly. McCarthey and Moje (2002: 231–2) assert:

> Identities [are the] clusters of stories that we tell about ourselves and others tell about us. . . . identities [are also] performed or enacted, rather than only told. . . . We live our identities in a sort of narrative, . . . searching for ways to construct or represent identities and stories that allow [us] to belong.

Explorations using various ICT also provided further evidence that the children's personal, social, cultural and textual worlds converge in play. Kendrick (2005: 9) noted that:

> When young children use the context of play as a medium for story-telling their social histories become interwoven into their play texts. The construction of such texts involves a continual interpretation and reinterpretation of their personal life experience in which children simultaneously represent reality and develop different modes of representing it.

The children's play with the camera became a time in which they could take control of the agenda and co-create their own narratives. They were able to use, manipulate and transform the social discourses and practices with which they were familiar in constructive and collaborative ways. As Haas Dyson (1997: 13) commented, children infuse their own intentions and their own meanings into the objects and actions of their play, and play therefore becomes a site for identity representation, formation and transformation.

ICT, multiliteracies and literacy learning

As previously indicated, literacy was viewed as social practice within this early learning centre. The concepts and processes inherent in a pedagogy of multi-literacies were embraced enthusiastically at the centre as it was seen to be an extension of text-based literacy that resonated with the philosophy and the pedagogical approaches used. Megan's observations indicate that children engaged in a range of experiences, modalities and texts and thus were showing competence in becoming multiliterate.

> We have also included more literacy with cooking – using a recipe book and following directions, then making our own documentation with text and images, and the same with science experiments. The children are very interested. They watch me write and want to add things and then watch me write what they have said and ask me to read it back. A few of the children had watched me fill the attendance roll and became interested. One of the children asked to do it [see Figure 5.2]. She had been watching me for a while. She then had a go. She noticed the repetition of the word Monday and asked about this.

Rather than traditional text-based literacies and multiliteracies being mutually exclusive, exposure to multiliterate contexts promoted interest in traditional practices associated with reading and writing. This is clearly shown in an extract from Megan's notes.

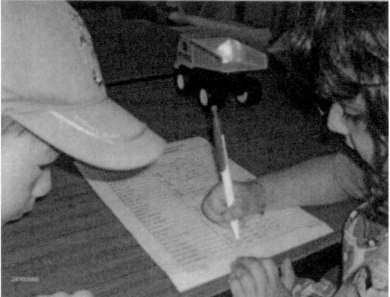

Figure 5.2 Practising text-based literacy skills in authentic contexts.

Early in the year Jane was writing down names on her clipboard and asking how to spell names she did not know how to write. Jane is an interested and self-motivated literacy learner. Jane has been experimenting with print and writing at our writing centre and has been practising at home. She started making books by drawing and then writing words and letters on each page. Jane is interested in the computer. She is confident to explore and ask questions about the programs. By exploring and experimenting with buttons and tools Jane quickly understands how to use the many different tools in the programs and independently use the software. Jane has been interested in the digital camera. She has made some movies and taken many photos of her friends.

Aspects of personal identity such as confidence and risk taking that had emerged through the use of technology were empowering for her and for Cody and flowed into their experimentation with writing. Megan noted that:

Cody shows confidence, leadership – ability to negotiate digital landscape, problem solve using his own knowledge – able to access further assistance when necessary – uses teacher only when necessary – self-directed. Cody and his friends were exploring tools and ideas that I hadn't shown them how to use. Cody became interested in learning to write his own name towards the end of the year. He was particularly motivated when he spent time with peers such as Jane that were exploring and experimenting with words. Cody has always loved to share a book with the teacher and is now exploring books with peers and independently. While Cody seemed to enjoy storybooks he is very interested in information books on dinosaurs and maps.

The focus on the processes of learning as well as the outcomes of learning was very significant for Megan. Her documentation of the children's learning and participation indicates that Cody and Jane were both active participants in the group, eager to share ideas, try new experiences and to experiment with new ideas and possibilities with peers.

Exploring audio

Due to her interest in multiliteracies, Megan also included exploration and experimentation with the software program called Super Duper Music Looper in her work with the children (Figure 5.3). Super Dooper Music Looper is designed to allow children to create their own music. It includes instrumental and diverse sound effects accompanied by visual symbols that children can explore and manipulate. This linking of aural and visual symbols is particularly

Figure 5.3 Exploring audio.

relevant to our thinking about linking modes of representation. The children were able to record their own vocals and accompaniments varying tempo, beat and style. Megan's notes describe the introduction of the music software to the children and their subsequent explorations of this audio aspect of multi-literacies. Over time the children also became more adept with utilising the possibilities of this literacy to communicate meaning to others.

June–September
Interest in the Super Dooper Music Looper emerged slowly. This is the story. The CD player in our room was broken so we used the computer to play music CDs for a couple of weeks. E was interested in where the sound was coming from and so I moved the speakers from inside the cabinet to the outside so the children could see them. The children began to ask questions about the speakers and hold them up to their ears to hear the sound. E held the speakers up and used the microphone to sing along to the music that was playing, other children picked up on this idea and we had lots of 'singalongs'. I suggested that we get a microphone to record our voices. We installed the microphone and the children began to experiment with recording their

voices. We used the Super Dooper Music Looper software to record and play the children's voices. Experimenting with the microphone led to interest in the other features of the program and the children began to explore and experiment.

October

Children now often choose to play with this program. S, E, Jane, K and Cody are all confident with choosing sounds and painting them on. Often children work together on this program (the sounds usually draw a crowd) and so the children have the opportunity to share their knowledge and ideas. Jane was the first to mix a track using the Super Dooper Music Looper program. I sat and showed her once how to add sounds and play the track and she picked it up straight away. She played it for her friends and we danced it together. Jane was very confident and mixed some great tracks to come up with a piece independently. She worked out how to play and stop the music as well as how to add additional sounds to the mixer.

Megan also noted that the children incorporated their new skills into existing literacy practices at the centre.

We're using sound effects in group time now. The children choose the books and we incorporate the sound effects into the story.

It became apparent that in working with Super Dooper Music Looper the children extended their repertoire of technological skills and created opportunities and contexts for becoming multiliterate. For example, they thought about sounds that would extend the meaning of a story, matched sounds with visual symbols and also were able to describe the music using descriptive language and kinaesthetic responses such as gesture and whole-body responses.

ICT, multiliteracies and identity

The use of ICT and the opportunity to become multiliterate supported both Jane and Cody, as well as other children in the group, in developing and demonstrating a strong sense of self and an ability to work collaboratively and creatively with others. The children in the centre were allowed the freedom to explore, and over time found new and innovative ways to interact with the software. The open-ended nature of the software enabled children to make their own meaning and determine the level of complexity they wanted. For Jane this allowed opportunities for independent, as well as collaborative work, and a level of complexity that was personally satisfying for her. Megan described the process of use of ICT and becoming multiliterate for Jane:

> She really liked making movies, organizing interviews and being interviewed. She always had great ideas and was a leader. She was also very creative in her drawing. I think she was a bit of an inspirational leader.

Traditional literacy practices of reading and writing can operate alongside explorations with multimedia and ICT, but constructing that relationship requires teachers to actively seek out new opportunities. Thoughtful observations of the children's playful responses can assist teachers to merge student's interests and ways of being with literacy learning and to help each child to recognize the ways literacy can contribute to their own personal goals and interests (Compton-Lilly 2006; Plowman and Stephen 2007). Megan provided some interesting examples:

> At one point the children became interested in the layout of the inside of a house. This led to an interest in house plans. The children then used the shape tool on Kid Pix to make the rooms. One of the children showed the others how to use the text tool. They then labelled the room using the text tool. An interest in making rainbows on the computer led to an interest in painting rainbows and it was the boys who took this up. An interest in keeping their work on the computer led to finding out how to save. C is saving his work in a file and typing his name.

In thinking about becoming multiliterate, it was evident that Megan valued opportunities for the children to be creative. This meant that some more unusual or idiosyncratic responses and personal aspects of identity were valued and regarded as legitimate in the classroom. Further, they were also apparent to parents who were then encouraged to make their own linking of various modes to support their children's literacy learning in informal ways in out-of-school contexts.

Dispositions to learning

Megan believed that the validation of children's interests and knowledge was also significant for the children's dispositions to learning such as motivation and engagement, persistence and risk taking. She commented that these dispositions were supported through her work with multiliteracies in ways which she felt would be less apparent when teachers relied on text-based worksheets in their 'readiness for school programmes'.

Challenging the labels of identity

The children's experiences with multimodal learning using ICT that is exemplified in the pedagogy of multiliteracies acted as a catalyst for teachers to look at the personal identity of children in new ways. During a meeting of the research team Megan commented:

> We had seen Cody as shy but Cody was able to feel 'big in his world' through making his Jurassic Park movie. He was not violent or aggressive or needing to intimidate others, but the movie meant that he was able to feel 'big' and 'powerful' and this also continued afterwards. The role play used his strengths, knowledge and skills of communication. Making movies about superhero play made it OK to be interested in something that is often banned at preschool, and we saw this interest being explored by different children and in new ways. Jane was shy too but she really liked making movies, organizing interviews and being interviewed. Both children were empowered and confident and used their initiative and creativity in ways that made sense for them. A multiliteracies framework enabled the children to use their many languages.

These comments demonstrate the hybridity and shifting nature of identity and challenge the practice of labelling children in a static way that is characterized by specific fixed attributes. Megan's comments suggest openness to different possibilities and the need to rethink and revise the labels that had previously been used to identify and talk about children. This resonates with McCarthey and Moje (2002: 230) who noted that new conceptualizations of identity have moved beyond not only the labelling

> but also the dichotomizing of possibilities for identity. One might argue that people can be both motivated and lazy, both aggressive and shy, depending on the spaces they are in and the relationships they enact within those spaces.

Collaborative learning and situated learning: communities of practice

Cody and Jane's experiences suggest that an educational environment that celebrated diverse responses and valued and supported observational learning and peer scaffolding enabled them to be successful literacy learners. Their interactions with each other and their use of ICT as an artefact for documenting and playing facilitated their learning and acted as a conduit for storytelling that was personal and relevant. The cases of Cody and Jane indicate that fears regarding children's isolation through ICT use are unfounded. In these scenarios the digital learning spaces were highly interactive where children learnt together by watching and listening to each other, by demonstrating, modelling and co-constructing knowledge (Figure 5.4). The children worked collaboratively, allowing space for the exploration of different interests and processes. The valuing of diversity in the classroom enabled the children to see the value in what others did, even if it was different from their own contribution. Verbal encouragement and scaffolding by the educators highlighted the advantages of this sharing of perspectives, knowledge and experience. For example:

> Today Cody sat with his friend at the computer and showed him how to use Kid Pix. He showed him how to make different things and how to edit the game. Cody has been a great teacher in the digital play space! He shows his friends different features of the program and helps his friends when they get stuck. Cody sometimes can't solve the problem, in which case he calls the teacher for help. The computer is so often a social experience for the children. We rarely see one child sitting alone at the computer and it's great to see children helping

Figure 5.4 Collaborative learning opportunities.

each other and interacting as they play the games. We can also see how the software is promoting skills for the children.

The work of Lave and Wenger (1990) on situated learning has relevance here. They describe the relational character of knowledge and learning and the ways in which meaning is negotiated by people who are actively engaged in solving relevant dilemmas in context. Learning is said to occur most effectively within 'communities of practice'. These communities bind their members together into a functional social group. The interactions that occur within a community of practice such as cooperation, problem solving, the building of trust and goodwill have the potential to build the networks and relationships of a community that enhance the well-being of the individuals within it.

And so to school . . .

The experiences of the two children at school were both similar and different. As previously stated, Cody was placed in a kindergarten class while Jane was placed in a composite class of kindergarten and Year 1 children. Our observations and those of their preschool teacher, Megan, suggested that while some aspects of pedagogy, timetable and curriculum were similar across the two classrooms, there were also some differences in the pedagogies used and the philosophical stance between the two teachers, and the impact that these had on their programme was evident.

Cody's experience in the kindergarten class at school, as with his preschool programme, offered him access to a range of play and learning resources as well as computer programs. The opportunities for access and use were, however, significantly different. Experiences of 'developmental play' or 'play as learning' within the kindergarten classroom appeared to be viewed as operating outside of the curriculum which was framed around key learning areas of English, maths, science, and human society and its environments.

In Cody's preschool experience, the children's ideas and directions were pivotal to the educational directions taken in the form of emergent curriculum. Now in this classroom context, curriculum outcomes and teacher direction were seen as the prime sources to drive learning. Play and children's interests featured for a short time period, generally in the afternoon, and were viewed as being outside the 'regular' literacy curriculum. The children in kindergarten participated in a literacy 'block' that occurred each morning for approximately an hour. The children were grouped in small groups of five or six children that rotated through different planned literacy activities, whilst the classroom teacher worked with a small group of children with similar literacy needs on a specifically identified aspect of literacy. Tasks included activities such as a worksheet on phonics, illustrating a story, a word-matching game that children completed independently. Within the school context, observations of Cody as a literacy learner revealed a somewhat different picture as the year progressed. Megan noted the following during her observation visit in Term 1:

> Cody is involved in independent sentence writing. He is in the top reading group. They are looking at question marks, italics, punctuation. He was writing words last year. He seems shy but confident. He is quiet by nature. Books were always an interest.

Later in the year the observations indicated a less confident child. Notes recorded during the second follow-up visit stated:

> Cody attends to each task as outlined by the teacher. He looks at his friend's page to check he has the right information. He looked at child next to him to check spelling. Cody seems to operate in the classroom in a much more covert way.

Megan's reflections on her observations focused on her observations of a 'different' child and she commented:

> This is not the Cody that we knew last year . . . In the preschool group Cody felt confident to negotiate the learning environment himself. Through sharing their experience with each other, Cody and Jane were able to share their knowledge and skills. They were each able to share with the others the aspects of the computer interaction that they discovered and enjoyed. This is very different to Cody's school experience where the need to be 'correct' seems pervasive. Cody seems to be unable to openly negotiate and construct meaning and experiences with his peers. He resorts to covert actions of secretly looking at other children's work to assure the correctness of his own. Learning (literacy) here is not a group experience but a reflection of individuals who are expected to work alone. He also seems to no longer feel able to access teacher help if he needs it. There is an emphasis on self, the individual, on getting it right – not group learning. Cody doesn't seem to feel capable of negotiating the learning environment like he did, say, with Kid Pix in the preschool group.

Cody's experience as a literacy learner at school again highlights the contextual nature of identity. Although initially (at preschool and in Term 1 of school) demonstrating a level of confidence with literacy tasks, this was not sustained. As the year at school progressed, in the context of more traditional text-based approaches to literacy accompanied by didactic pedagogical approaches, his desire not to make mistakes and conform to the task at hand seemed to have the effect of eroding his confidence and subduing his performance and personality. During a team meeting for our project this issue was discussed further and the following comments were made by Megan (his former preschool teacher):

> Cody seems lost and a shadow of who he was – he used to have opportunities, make decisions, be more himself, . . . – not just academic expectations. Our valuing of his ideas gave him a chance to find his voice and creativity e.g. his video where he planned, developed and produced his own short video entitled 'Jurassic Park'. This experience had helped him to be big in the world of the preschool. There were no set outcomes and there were different premises, a different philosophy as foundation. I think he felt safe. He was given opportunities to be himself. Our environment fostered his independence – he was seen as important. We have an expectation that they [the children] can and will lead their own learning. We value and encourage independence in learning and we value the process of participation. We are trying to give them a voice. There are no set and restrictive pressures and so creativity emerges and creativity breeds creativity. You can create a culture that breeds one thing or another. His school experience is very outcome, worksheet focused and he seems very quiet, compliant and less rather than more than what we used to see.

The educators at the early childhood centre discussed how the kindergarten programme at school and the preschool programme differed. The discussion included the following synthesis by Megan:

> We value that children learn in different ways. It is about identifying and valuing. I think there is a greater openness to the child and we genuinely value and seek their input. We work hard to create an environment of ownership and empowerment and respect. We have a joint team approach to learning – not them and us – which it seems to be at school. I think for us it is 'in order to make this work I have to listen to you and hear you'. The curriculum for us emerges from the children by genuine response to their interest and decision-making. We offer open-ended experiences and then the children are prepared to take risks. There is freedom to achieve in terms of where it goes.

The early school experiences of Jane provided a much more positive picture. During the first observation visit the following was noted by Megan:

> Jane appears very independent in her work in the classroom. She uses the dictionary to answer her own questions regarding spelling. She is observing others but doesn't appear to need or want any help. She seems able and very happy to operate on her own level. There is evidence of child choice and Jane seems able to use the strengths we saw last year.

This was maintained, and later in the year the notes from our observations indicated:

> There is a shared reading experience with the book *Whistle up the Chimney*. In literacy groups Jane does a painting in response to the story. 'I'm doing the express train', Jane says. The boy next to her responds with, 'You don't know how to do expresses.' Jane continues her painting without comment. After Jane finishes her painting she writes about it. 'The express train coming out of the chimney.' Jane stops. She notices another child near her who is not sure what to do on the computer. He is trying to log on. Jane says 'Write anything. S, I'll help you.' Jane types the child's name in the log on box and says 'now you press Next.'

This observation and the more general observations undertaken within Jane's classroom indicated greater consistency between the pedagogical approaches adopted within the early childhood centre and the school that continued beyond the first term of the school year. Observations of the work displayed in this classroom indicated that children were provided with many opportunities for creative responses using a range of different media. Megan noted a number of similarities to the work which the children had undertaken during the previous year in her preschool programme. These included: children's written stories accompanied by children's paintings, drawings and constructions, and options given for children to respond to experiences in ways that were personally meaningful, and the graphic representation of brainstorming or webbing of the children's ideas and responses. The webbing of children's ideas and knowledge in relation to the topic for discussion (Figure 5.5) was similar to webbing used for emergent curriculum by some early childhood educators in prior to preschool settings (Arthur *et al.* 2005: 185–6; Katz and Chard 2000).

The mixed-age grouping of the composite class could have provided the catalyst for the use of the specific pedagogical approaches with which Jane was familiar, such as small interest-based groups, and more open-ended tasks. When similar approaches were evident within the school context Jane appeared to grow in confidence, and was able to extend her skills in creativity, problem solving and collaboration.

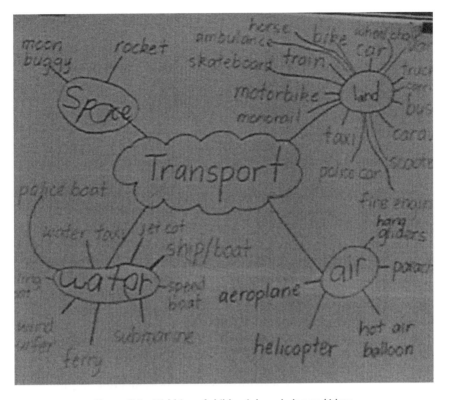

Figure 5.5 Webbing of children's knowledge and ideas.

The link between identity and expectations within a particular cultural context is reinforced through these two cases. Ways of knowing, doing, believing, acting, reading and writing are discourses that are tied to the cultural models by which people live (Gee 1996) and through which classrooms operate. These discourses, which are embedded in classroom practices, also shape children's identities and identifications. As McCarthey and Moje (2002: 231) assert:

> The link between cultural models and identities is important. Identities are at least in part culturally situated, mediated, and constructed. They are not solely an innate quality that children are born with ... Identities are built within the social interactions one has within a particular Discourse community.

Multiliteracies and transitions

Although there are many factors which determine school success when peda-gogical approaches were more consistent between the early childhood and school contexts, the outcomes for Jane appeared to be more positive and her strengths, evident within the preschool year, sustained. Cody's placement in the kindergarten class where the teacher's approaches, philosophies and prior-ities differed more significantly from those of his preschool experience created greater discontinuity for Cody between his preschool experience and that of being in school. Ultimately, it seemed to disorientate him and cause a loss of confidence in himself as a literacy learner.

The classroom environment for Cody was typical of many school class-rooms and reflected an educational context where product, assessment, out-comes and benchmarks become the primary determinants of teaching practice. It would seem that, as Haas Dyson (2003) suggests, schools primarily focus on helping students to manipulate the written symbols of the culture in ways that are academically and socially valued within the institution of formal school-ing. It is also these forms of literacy that are gaining greater priority as they are increasingly being used within systems of teacher accountability as measures of teacher effectiveness. Rather than the focus on interdependence and col-laboration of the preschool, the priority became individual work designed to meet the set outcomes within the key learning areas: 'literacy and literate practices are tools for representing or performing particular identities ... literacy practices ... [can constrain] identity representations and [position] them in particular ways' (McCarthey and Moje 2002: 231).

The strengths-based approach used in the preschool group which drew on Cody's existing knowledge and skills (as a 3- and 4-year-old) and helped Cody to flourish appeared to be replaced (at age 5) by a 'needs-based' approach. This needs-based approach was evident in the focus on what these children needed to know, what they needed to be taught in order to meet the outcomes. Both these factors seemed to impact on Cody's identity as a learner and ultimately decreased his confidence and ability to take risks. The need to meet text-based literacy outcomes and the use of these as measures of teacher effectiveness create pressure for teachers. Literacy learning at school was narrowed to text-based literacy that was focused on reading, writing and spelling. It did not encourage children to extend and explore other forms of language and communication nor demonstrate their expertise with ICT. Their skills in being multiliterate, so evident in their preschool year, were not apparent. This reflects Haas Dyson's (2003: 5) claim that the tendency to focus on text-based literacy means that children's cultural worlds, and the breadth of their textual experience, the depth of their social and symbolic adaptability, disappear.

The differences and (physical) separation between early childhood and primary education (Sawyer 2000) are easy to identify. Britt and Sumsion (2002) also argue that there is a tendency in much of the research to place early childhood education and primary education within a dichotomous conceptual order whereby the focus is on differences, separation, binary opposition and mutual exclusivity – the either/or framework. The pedagogy of multiliteracies provide a context for what Britt and Sumsion call 'border crossing' in which new and possibly different languages, cultures and landscapes are negotiated. This seemed much more evident in the case of Jane where continuity in pedagogical approaches was more apparent. Jane continued to take risks, seek challenges and flourish as a multiliterate learner building on aspects of identity previously developed.

Jane's placement in a kindergarten – Year 1 composite class appeared advantageous as the mixed age group required more differentiation of the curriculum, more open-ended tasks and the grouping of children based on their strengths and abilities. The teacher of this class had a degree in early childhood education and had come to the school environment after recent work experience within a long daycare environment and was therefore more familiar with the pedagogical approaches that Jane had experienced within the early learning centre. As Comber (1997: 3) comments:

> Through examining how children's knowledges and practices count in school life or not we can design workable responsive and inclusive curricula. At the same time further examination of the pedagogical practices of highly effective early childhood teachers has much to offer as we reconceptualise curricula and reinvent pedagogies for new times.

A multiliteracies framework and associated pedagogy offers an alternative view of literacy learning and can add to existing approaches and frameworks operating within both early childhood and school settings.

Summary

The experiences of Cody and Jane outlined in this chapter illustrate the ways in which learners respond to different approaches to literacy teaching and learning. They highlight the powerful ways in which teachers can affect children's self-efficacy and ultimately their literacy preferences and performance. The pedagogy of multiliteracies can effectively support the self-expression, creativity and problem solving of learners as well as the relational qualities of identity. While schools operate within their own particular constraints and requirements and shared ways of communicating, such as spelling and grammar, the results of this project indicate that a pedagogy of multiliteracies can contribute to learning and teaching in the early years in contemporary times.

The pedagogy of multiliteracies can extend literacy learning, allowing children to become confident, to be able to take risks and to share their ideas, knowledge and skills with others. It can extend cooperation and collaboration and in turn foster a climate of interdependence. The focus on processes as well as outcomes of learning can build and sustain a community of learners characterized by curiosity, confidence and eagerness to participate in new opportunities for discovery and collaboration.

6 Engaging with diversity

Introduction

This chapter focuses on how teachers can reflect on issues around diversity so that they are able to support children's individual strengths, areas of potential, and use their preferred ways of learning to engage, extend and increase their repertoire of skills. It explores the ways in which this might be achieved utilizing the pedagogy of multiliteracies and via the incorporation of ICT in learning experiences. As stated in Chapter 4, we contend that viewing children as multimodal learners in a digital world enables educators to cater more effectively for individual learners.

In this chapter, we present and discuss the cases of Brendan and Charlotte to illustrate the ways in which the pedagogy of multiliteracies assisted their teachers to transform both their perceptions of children with special needs, and their planning of new learning experiences for them. We realized that such shifts in perceptions and pedagogy resulted in a greater respect for the diverse strengths and interests of children. It also highlighted the place of diversity and difference within dynamic and contemporary early childhood learning communities. Teachers broadened their vision of diversity when observing and documenting children's learning and while collaborating with children and families. Their new understandings informed the design and implementation of new learning experiences and environments. As time progressed it became apparent that the teachers were increasingly committed to ensuring that they were responsive to the children's diverse abilities, interests and lifeworlds in order to meet the special needs of each child in a variety of ways. These changes generated a new attitude towards learning that was grounded in belonging and transformation and was sensitive to the diversity that characterized the children in their care. This, in turn, strengthened the relationships and connections between children, educators and families within their early childhood learning community.

Challenges and contradictions

Valuing and respecting diversity and difference has a long-standing recognition in early childhood education (Cannella 1997; Creaser and Dau 1996; Robinson and Jones Díaz 2006). This is evident, for example, in *Anti-Bias Curriculum* (Derman-Sparkes and the ABC Task Force 1989), and within a range of Australian early childhood policy and curriculum documents that had particular relevance for the teachers participating in the project such the *NSW Curriculum Framework – The Practice of Relationships* (NSW Office of Child Care 2002) and *Early Childhood Code of Ethics* (Early Childhood Australia 2007). In addition, these documents recognize the importance of the early years for establishing a sense of identity and belonging and for supporting the development of values of social justice and fairness for all, regardless of socio-economic status, age, gender, race, language and ability.

This commitment to diversity and difference, social justice and equity is, however, one discourse among many operating within contemporary early childhood education and one which is under threat in contemporary times. In recent years the neo-liberal agenda which focuses on the individual, government surveillance and intervention in education policy, has also impacted on early childhood care and education. Bronwyn Davies, in the preface to Robinson and Jones Díaz (2006: xii) commented: 'Those dominant, neoliberal discourses that homogenize students and instil competitive individualism in students, aggressively undermining strategies of inclusion and the valuing of difference and diversity, currently have enormous power'. Aspects of accountability and compliance have gained increasing influence throughout the community and impacted on the care and education of its youngest members. This is evident in regulatory requirements, legal liability and discussions of assessment of professional performance. Early childhood educators frequently comment on the imposition of external agendas and their diminishing professional autonomy (Sumsion 2006).

The neo-liberal focus on education for workplace productivity is evident in externally imposed requirements for the standardized assessment of literacy and numeracy in the early years. Academically rated individual performance in relation to traditional text-based literacy is increasingly becoming the priority for many teachers within the first years of school (e.g. Good Start, NSW). This grading of young children in literacy has a significant impact on educational programmes in the early years of school as well as having a flow-down effect into the educational programmes offered to children prior to school. Early assessment using standardized measures can shift the focus of both pedagogy and curriculum to homogeneity and result in difference being seen as problematic rather than as an opportunity for new learning and ways of understanding. The introduction of formal standardized testing to younger children can also generate parental concern about their children's success on standardized literacy tests in the early years of school and expectations for formal literacy learning for younger and younger children. Parents at times expect to see evidence of early literacy and numeracy milestones and outcomes and within 'readiness for school programmes' in preschools and daycare environments (Dockett and Perry 2007). This can reduce the opportunities for educators to build on the linguistic and cultural diversity evident within their learning community as the foundation for developing additional literacy and numeracy skills and understandings.

Within discourses of neo-liberalism and neo-conservatism there is an increased emphasis on the dominant culture and a decreasing recognition of the value of the cultural and linguistic and social identities of children and their families. For example, parents of bilingual children, rather than being supported to recognize the value of their home language use, can feel pressured to strengthen the child's use of the majority language at the expense of the home language. Jones Díaz comments: 'Despite the fact that people around the world desire to pass on to their children the language through which local identities are expressed, families are under considerable pressure to abandon their home language or dialect in favour of English (Robinson and Jones Díaz, 2006: 107).

Difference in relation to social life has also been marginalized through the discourses of childhood innocence and vulnerability that have gained influence within neo-liberal and neo-conservative agendas. The increased surveillance of young children within the community and the protection of children from harm have been used to promote normalizing discourses of family and community life (Robinson and Jones Díaz 2006). Within a discourse of homogeneity and normalization, difference is 'othered' or seen as a threat or danger, with children needing protection so that their innocence is preserved. This protection of childhood innocence has been used to justify the exclusion of others and denies all children access to the complexity of living in contemporary times. It also denies the reality of the diversity and complexity of childhood experience. Childhood is not one universalized experience of growing up within 'happy, homogenous families', rather children are members of diverse family types as well as citizens of their local and the globalized world. They are therefore exposed, to varying degrees, to the diversity of human experience. This diversity includes demographic aspects such as gender, age, ethnicity/race, locale, socio-economic group and disability, as well as the diversity of lifeworlds which includes experience, interests, orientations, values, faith, dispositions, sensibilities, communication and interpersonal styles and thinking styles (New London Group 1996). While educators may be aware of and responsive to the broad demographics of their respective learning communities, the increasing dominance of discourses of normalization and protection of childhood innocence can reduce the opportunities for in-depth discussion and investigation of aspects of diversity and difference with children, colleagues and families and reinforce the operation of stereotypes and bias.

Multiliteracies and diversity

As outlined in Chapter 2, the research which informs this book was located within the context of the complexities and contradictions associated with the place of diversity within early childhood education. Fundamental to the research objectives, design and methodology was a commitment to diversity and difference and social justice perspectives. The project objectives were designed to facilitate the inclusion of marginalized groups within the community and provide support for diversity and difference within early learning contexts. Participation in the project involved teachers in identifying and investigating the extent of the impact of early access to ICT and the value of multiliteracies in relation to the learning profiles of children in families from low socio-economic areas, minority and disadvantaged groups, including Indigenous children, children from language backgrounds other than English and children with special needs. The project enabled teachers and children in low socio-economic areas to gain access to the advanced educational technologies assisting in closing the gap between the ICT 'rich' and the ICT 'poor'. The use of ICT and the adoption of a multiliteracies perspective on early literacy learning provided validation for the participant teachers in their attempts to honour and respect diversity in their daily work. The design and implementation of the multiliteracies profile, pedagogies and pathways described in Chapter 7 was a result of listening to teachers as they went about their daily work and considered the essential information that they needed to know about the diverse individuals in their care.

In working with the teachers, it became apparent that teaching and learning within the multiliteracies profile, pedagogies and pathways framework meant that aspects of the personal, social and cultural experiences of young children, which may have been overlooked or seen as deficits within traditional understandings of language and literacy learning, were reconceptualized as assets that could be identified, extended and shared with others in ways which transformed learning and teaching for both adults and children. Essential to multiliteracies thinking is valuing diversity and difference and the pedagogical approaches that support diversity by focusing on processes, relationships and dispositions as well as outcomes. The New London Group (1996) suggested that:

> The term 'multiliteracies' refers to two major aspects of language use today. The first is the variability of meaning making in different

cultural, social or professional contexts. As much as English is becoming a global language, these differences are becoming ever more significant to our communications environment. The second is the nature of new communications technologies. Meaning is made in ways that are increasingly multimodal – in which written-linguistic modes of meaning interface with visual, audio, gestural and spatial patterns of meaning.

In the field of early childhood education, Viruru (2001: 39) has recommended that:

> If we wish to reconceptualise early childhood education as a field that creates increased opportunities for younger human beings it would appear essential that we create spaces for children to explore and employ multiple forms of communication.

As noted in Chapter 1, catering for diversity is an essential component of contemporary education and the key to successful schooling experiences for students. If we are able to connect to children's lifeworlds they will be able to contextualize their learning and make the process more fluid and engaging. The notion of 'one size fits all' is obsolete and in 'doing diversity' in schools we need to be aware of the fundamental role that families and the community share to promote the learning of children from a wide range of backgrounds.

The cases

As previously indicated, diversity encompasses many aspects, and one aspect of diversity is not generalizable to the many aspects of diversity. Similarly, each context is a unique combination of factors and each learner is an individual, not representative of all learners of 'that kind'. However, while not wishing to generalize from each case to the wider population, the pedagogical approaches outlined have relevance beyond the specifics.

The cases in this chapter explore the early learning experiences of children participating in an early intervention programme for children with additional needs and rights located within a socially disadvantaged area. In particular, they describe two children identified as children with autism spectrum disorder (ASD) and language delay who are often further marginalized in educational contexts. Examples from these cases are used to highlight the diverse capabilities and experiences that young children bring to early learning environments such as daycare and preschool. The observations and reflections of teachers illustrate the ways in which they have explored aspects of contemporary early childhood pedagogy in designing learning experiences and environments to meet the special needs and capacities of individual learners in a variety of ways. In particular, the cases provide insight to the place of multi-literacies and ICT within a strengths-based and collaborative pedagogy and the implications for children who are socially and economically disadvantaged and those with ASD and language delay. The comments provided are drawn from the observations, discussions and the reflective journals of Chris, the director of the early intervention programme within the preschool. Her thoughtful observations, collaborative discussions and analysis were vital to the investigation and substantiate the importance of the time for research and reflection within educational settings.

Background

Brendan and Charlotte were participants in an early intervention programme located within a community-based preschool for children aged 3–5 years. The preschool is located in an outer suburban area of Sydney with a high level of public housing and socio-economic disadvantage. Brendan and Charlotte attended the programme for 2 days each week. Both children are Anglo-Australian and have been diagnosed with ASD and delayed language. At age 5, Brendan began his enrolment in kindergarten at a special school for children with high support needs, while Charlotte continued for another year within the programme at the early intervention service and a year later entered a class for children with ASD in a mainstream school.

Pedagogy at the preschool

The early intervention programme at the preschool is founded on socioconstructivist approaches and emphasizes the importance of peer learning. The programme for children with additional needs operates within the mainstream preschool programme, acknowledging the importance of the social interactions and learning that occurs within peer relationships. The teachers at the centre draw on a number of approaches such as postmodern perspectives and anti-bias in their work with children and families. Brendan and Charlotte participated actively in a full-day programme of play and learning experiences within the indoor and outdoor environments. Like Cody's school (see page 86), Brendan and Charlotte enjoyed a mixture of traditional play resources alongside technology such as a computer, DVD and CD players.

A strengths-based approach

The early intervention programme provides a play-based approach to learning and skill development. Children with additional needs are integrated into the mainstream educational program and educators observe each child closely to identify their strengths and interests as a basis for curriculum planning, interactions and intervention. The programme provided for the children is founded on the principles of the state curriculum framework (NSW Office of Child Care 2002). This curriculum framework views all children as strong, resourceful and capable, and so every effort is made by teachers to identify all children's strengths and preferred modes of learning. The use of ICT has a valued place within this strengths-based approach to diversity and difference, and the place of multiliteracies was explored within this context.

The play and learning experiences offered to children build on the strengths and interests of the children as well as their lived experiences within their families and communities. Parent communication is crucial to the programme and parents' knowledge of children is actively sought. Chris noted:

> In a strengths based and collaborative approach we don't just ask parents about needs and deficits. We want to know about children's interests, their loves and their strengths. It is about asking the parents and getting their feedback. So when staff say that we have noticed that she loves music videos, we get the parent response – 'Yes, as you said, she loves this, she loves music videos.' Then we invite the parent to write some relevant information about what happens at home and that comes back in to the preschool and we work with that new knowledge about the child. So it really is an experience linked with the family experience. We acknowledge the place of the child in the family and the role of the parent in the child's life and the link or the partnership we have with the parents of the children. And parents feel that they are working with us in a valued way. They are thrilled that we believe their child has strengths and interests as well as the many areas of difficulty. So much of their experience with their child is challenging and more focused on the hard work of developing functional skills. You can see their relief when we are focusing on the positives that the child already has. We use the stuff the child can do and we see their joy that someone else can see this in their child and value and use it too.

Approaches to literacy learning

Links with families and communities are also evident in approaches to text-based literacy learning. The educator's work in the area of literacy is founded on an understanding of literacy as social practice (Makin *et al.* 2007). Literacy practices evident in the home context are supported with the provision of culturally relevant resources and experiences such as newspapers in a range of scripts, junk mail, magazines, TV guides and bus timetables. The introduction of multiliteracies was an extension of this social practice approach to literacy and offered different spaces and new lenses through which teachers could view children's responses. This was evident in both planning of experiences and discussions with the children in relation to popular culture, food packaging and merchandising that were relevant to and meaningful within the children's daily lives. Chris talked about the work that she and her colleague Kym (the director of the mainstream preschool) undertook in relation to this:

> We have been looking at the packaging of the Neopet. The Neopet is the soft toy that comes with the Happy Meal and it is a very familiar aspect of the children's lives. We asked the children to make a guess about what Neopet might be in the packaging and so on . . . In looking at the packaging we were looking at visual text as well as written text. We often talk to the children about the pictures and I always say pictures give clues about what the words are about, what is trying to be conveyed by the packaging. Children can read these visual clues as a guide to what the words are about and what the packaging is telling us. They know that it is from McDonald's, from 'the Big M'. They are more able to use their own life knowledge and experience within a multiliteracies framework. We suggested that they could create their own Neopet and their responses were quite complex and they were focused and more socially together.

Critical literacies

Teachers at the centre have also developed a strong commitment to critical literacy as a way of empowering children and families within this community. Home and community experiences were also used as the context for the development of critical literacies. Chris recalled:

> I brought in two different packets of cornflakes – two different brands. We looked at the pictures on each box to gain clues of what might be inside each box. One box had cornflakes – so the children said 'cornflakes are in that box' and they opened it and that confirmed their idea. When they looked at the other box they could see a bowl with cornflakes with strawberries and milk being poured and a toy. We talked about what would be in the box and they thought that there should be cornflakes, strawberries and the toy. They were very excited to open the box and found the cornflakes and the toy. They were disappointed that they didn't find any strawberries. The children said 'if it is on the box it should be in the box' and that 'no strawberries is not fair.' This led to a very interesting conversation about why the strawberries were on the box and the concept of marketing and 'fair trade'.

The role of ICT

The teachers found that the use of the computer facilitates social interaction for children with ASD and language delay and supports those with challenging behaviours. Through careful observation and collaborative reflection the teachers realized that the physical layout of four chairs at the computer actually scaffolds the turn-taking process for children who generally find awareness of others, social conventions and social connections with peers very difficult. The absence or severe limitation of verbal language available to these children exacerbates the difficulties associated with social interaction, and so learning within the complex social context of play at the preschool can be highly problematic. Chris describes this aspect of her programme:

> The computer itself sets up the social setting. The layout of the chairs clarifies the turn-taking procedure. It helps them to know whose turn it is and when it will be their turn. This is so important as these children are highly distractible and easily frustrated. The wall chart of names for turns also provides a visible reflection of how the turn taking occurs. The children can move their name or picture along the board as their turn approaches and so they actively participate in this process. This physical involvement uses the children's constant seeking of sensory stimulation and need to move in a positive and functional way.

The teachers followed this up by creating a social story for the children that included visual images and text of the turn-taking process at the computer (Figure 6.1). By more consciously scaffolding the turn-taking process using a variety of modes, for example with printed text, using visual images, and assisting the child to move from last chair to first, the teachers enabled children with additional needs and their peers to be more aware of and responsive to the social practices associated with playing and learning with others. The practice of looking, waiting, sharing and turn taking became more overt and simplified for the children when they were using the computer. They learnt to look to see if there was a space to enter the play, to wait and to follow the social conventions associated with computer use and, with support, were able to transfer this knowledge to other situations. Chris's comments highlight this process:

> This physical and social space supported the development of social skills and awareness of others that was not possible for these children within the more complex and unstructured context of the traditional free play areas such as block play or dramatic play. We were then able to support the children to transfer the skills developed at the computer

Turn Taking On Our
Computer

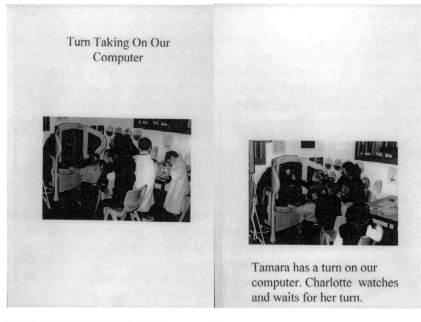

Tamara has a turn on our
computer. Charlotte watches
and waits for her turn.

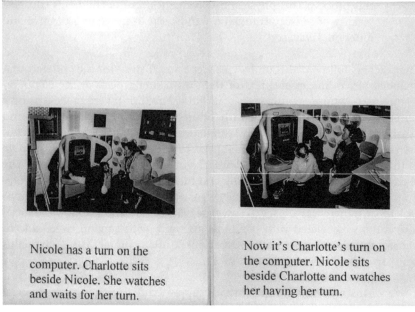

Nicole has a turn on the
computer. Charlotte sits
beside Nicole. She watches
and waits for her turn.

Now it's Charlotte's turn on
the computer. Nicole sits
beside Charlotte and watches
her having her turn.

Figure 6.1 A social story supports turn taking at the computer.

to other areas of the play and learning environment. Brendan and Charlotte, as well as the other children, began to use and respond to the visual, auditory, spatial and gestural cues associated with positive social interaction which is key to an inclusive programme.

Literacy learning at preschool

The educators in the early intervention programme and mainstream preschool found that ICT and the pedagogy of multiliteracies for literacy learning were very effective for all children at the centre and, in particular, those with ASD and language delay. Chris's journal reflections provide a powerful evidence of this. For example, she wrote:

> This year their competency improved. They are all using the computer programs. Quite a few of the older ones are going onto the keyboard, accessing letters. They are starting to read the alphabet letters, the pictures . . . more the sort of thing that you would be thinking they would be doing next year. A few of the older ones are getting into that, as well as one of the children from my programme with autism. Charlotte knows all the alphabet letters and can read many sight words. She can use the computer disk quite competently. The programs have got things like 'Put the dog beside the kennel.' She will know 'beside' and she is experiencing that sense of success, and the feedback of success . . . The program makes a little musical sound and so she gets that auditory feedback repeatedly. The repetition that these children need is legitimate when using computer.
>
> I think many parents with children with autism realize that they have a particular skill with numbers and words . . . and therefore they have a computer at home. We are finding ways to integrate the computer with other aspects of the literacy programme. We even looked at the location and shifted the computer to a quiet and inviting place near the foyer and close to the literacy area so play on the computer can easily lead through to the other literacy experiences that are right near [see Figure 6.2].

The organization of the physical environment reinforced the possible links between the computer and other literacy experiences, and children were encouraged to transfer their interest in letters, numbers and words and popular culture DVDs from the computer to their work with pencils and paper and use of books. The availability of magazines and shopping catalogues that were familiar aspects of the children's worlds also helped children to connect the letters, numbers and words on the screen to the text which appeared within these resources.

Figure 6.2 The location of computer near the book area enables the children to extend their interest in popular culture to text-based literacy resources.

Scaffolding learning

The educators in the early intervention programme have a strong commitment to scaffolding children's learning and so were conscious of and responsive to opportunities for helping children to make links and connections. Professional development for the team and participation in the research project have increased awareness of the importance of active adult participation in children's play and learning. This is evident in more thoughtful observation and active listening as a basis for any subsequent interactions. Rather than standing back or stepping in too rapidly, teachers were able to be more in tune with the child's agenda. Physical, gestural, visual and or verbal support was increasingly offered through prompts and questions that scaffolded the children's learning and enabled them to move within and to extend their zone of proximal development. Teaching and learning strategies focused on utilizing existing strengths and interests to support areas of emerging development using the ideas inherent in a pedagogy of multiliteracies.

In the case of Brendan and Charlotte, these interventions and provisions focused primarily on the development of oral and symbolic language through use of ICT and multimodal support for positive social interaction and awareness of peers. Chris provides some further insight into these developments:

> Recent staff training has helped – integrating literacy experience with children's play throughout the day has helped so our interactions throughout the whole day are more informed. We are reading stories differently and looking at aspects that support our children's strengths such as repetition and looking more at pictures. The team acknowledges the importance of literacy and what we do in a whole range of areas. Literacy links through the experience of language and in other parts of the programme such as dramatic play and sensory play. All educators are now more aware. You can't be available to it if you aren't aware of it and what you are able to support and how. When we have a child at the computer we usually have a staff member sitting beside the child, supporting or prompting the child and also to encourage those children in social aspects and shared problem solving. Computer time isn't hands-off time but hands-on time for teachers. It is a time to be there watching, listening and helping children to make the most of the experience across different developmental and curriculum areas.

Multiliteracies and collaborative learning in preschool

One of the key issues for children with ASD and language delay is the difficulty associated with being an effectively integrated and participating member of a social group. Social interactions and the reading of social cues are often highly problematic for these children, and so early intervention often has social relationships as a primary focus. While some programmes for children with ASD focus on withdrawing them for social skills training (Batchelor and Taylor 2005), the focus in the early intervention programme within this preschool was on developing social awareness through supported inclusion and scaffolded engagement with others in authentic contexts. The educators found that using ICT associated with the computer and multiliteracies supported genuine inclusion. A multimodal approach to learning, involving the use of linguistic, visual, audio, gestural and spatial cues, helped to introduce the children to specific types of communication and social relationships and strengthened social interaction and collaborative approaches to learning (Figure 6.3). Chris shared this process in a research meeting:

> We have noticed that Charlotte and Brendan are developing inter-personal skills while at the computer. Interactions are now happening. There is eye contact and vocalizations such as sound effects, utterances and some verbalizations. The visual cues within the programme, rather than promoting solitary participation, support this process. The auditory aspects, the sound effects and words help to sustain interest. And in relation to awareness of emotion, which is a big issue for these children, the repetition and humour is there. The children with ASD respond to this aspect on the computer when they see others laugh and begin to laugh too. The computer scaffolds connections and our ASD children offer advice to others, point,

Figure 6.3 Playing and learning at the computer encourages diverse forms of communication.

make utterances, use other gestures, and bounce up and down with enthusiasm.

In this context all the children in the class learned to sign and to use Board-maker pictures. This facilitated communication at all levels, and those children with additional needs were included in scenarios that they would have previously been excluded from as well as having the impact of reducing situations of conflict and misunderstanding between the children. The children with ASD became more aware of the other children in their class and were able at times to take the lead when proficiency with the computer enabled them to scaffold the learning of others (Figure 6.4).

As teachers moved from a deficit view to working with the children's strengths, they saw opportunities to use hitherto unrecognized aspects of the child's learning profile to strengthen others that were areas of difficulty for these children. The ability to experience and respond to emotion, so problematic for these children, was strengthened through the use of the computer program. Chris described how she built on the humour evident in the computer program to help the children to develop awareness of emotion within interactions and relationships with others:

> We use a (real) tickle in association with 'funny' so that the children begin to associate laughter with funny aspects. I build on the humour within the program and link this to the real interaction of a tickle and can do this over and over. The children with ASD are now seeking this form of physical and emotional interaction with us – which is a big milestone for them.

Social skills and communication processes explored with children in the non-threatening environment were explored in other aspects of the program and strengths evident in one learning centre were utilized to empower children in another. Chris explained:

> We also link our group time back to the shared experience of the computer and this provides a link for the children with ASD, language delay and the typically developing children. We do singing using Boardmaker and the children have the opportunity to use the concepts from the computer. Charlotte transferred her understanding of faster and slower on the computer to the group singing context. She was able to verbalize 'faster' or 'slower' to direct the group singing.
>
> We have also introduced chairs for our group time to again link to the social aspects of the computer. We have found that children would often previously avoid or resist group time as this is a social context which is often stressful because other children are in close

Figure 6.4 Teacher scaffolding enables children to transfer the social skills and turn taking developed at the computer to more formal learning situations. The children began to include the skills and practices from group time within their own self-initiated play and interaction.

physical proximity. Now the children with ASD are keener to participate and are coping better with the group time expectations of turn taking and looking forwards because of the familiarization and practice with chairs and the physical layout of the environment at the computer. This will assist them with the transition to the more formal context of school.

Multiliteracies and meaning making

Teachers also became more aware of and responsive to the ways in which children with different learning profiles make meaning from their experiences. This involved observing and understanding their diverse expressions of literacy and using the literacy of social practice within the children's own worlds rather than redirecting them to more traditional forms of language use and literacy learning. For examples, Chris noted:

> Brendan loved the Brio train set at preschool and he brought in his much cherished *Thomas the Tank Engine* DVD from home. We used this as an opportunity to build shared connections as well as literacy learning. We explained to the children that later in the day we would watch the DVD. We talked about going to the movies and what happens and what you need. Some children then wanted to make tickets and so they cut up paper and some added letters and numbers and others drew pictures of trains. Another child was interested in the food at the movies and said 'We need popcorn!' and so we made some popcorn and the children helped put this in paper bags for later. At the end of the day the children were invited to come to the movies if they wanted to. Some of the children helped the teachers to set up chairs in rows. The tickets were distributed to those what wanted to go. We lowered the blinds to reduce the light and then asked the children to hand in their tickets. At times these roles were undertaken by the children and the smell of the popcorn and the physical environment helped to create an atmosphere of excitement. The children were captivated by the experience and some didn't want to leave when their parents arrived to take them home. These parents then delayed going and joined in the experience.

This example demonstrates how the pedagogy of multiliteracies and using ICT helped the teachers to see the opportunities for meaning making that many children bring from their own lived experiences. They worked with what was meaningful for children and extended it. They modified their own agendas, space and style and became more attuned to the rhythms and complexities of the children's ideas, playful responses and interactions. As Paley (1990: 34) noted, 'an idea must find the rhythm of the group to be fully communicated'.

This active engagement in meaning making through multiliteracies was also evident in the ways in which the children from the mainstream preschool programme also used the ideas and approaches used with children with additional needs. Chris reflected on this observation:

> The use of the visuals initially designed to support the children with ASD and language delay has been embraced by all the children. The Boardmaker song pictures used at group time by the teacher were spontaneously incorporated into their play at other times. Children with or without additional needs will gather as a small group and use the visuals within a singing experience, sharing the roles of leaders and/or followers.

The children's willingness and desire for such highly complex social interaction challenged teacher's existing conceptions of the children. Chris commented that at times like these she viewed her role as subsidiary, and she tended to stay in the background to observe the children but would be readily available to support them in their activities if they called upon her.

In the year that followed Charlotte was able to take an increasingly cooperative role in play with her peers. She was observed at times to undertake the role of teacher using the various multimodal materials that could be found in the preschool, such as Boardmaker pictures, songs, and making decisions about the positioning of chairs as well as repeating the words and phrases typically used by the teacher at shared group times (Figure 6.5). This was very significant for Charlotte as she had in the past been isolated in her play world and her language had generally been limited to one word utterances or repetitive functional social speech such as 'hello', 'thank you', and 'more please'. As her teachers and parents observed this growth in Charlotte, they felt more confident about her transition to school.

Literacy learning at school

When he was 5 years old, Brendan started school and entered the kindergarten class at a special school for children with high support needs. Observations at the school were undertaken as part of the research project and involved visits by his preschool teacher and the researcher. These observations were then shared with the group in the research circles. Chris's initial observations were of the literacy learning time. For example, she wrote:

> Brendan selects the sign for cold – and places on board. The teacher initiates the chant 'Today is Tuesday' and Brendan sings 'Toast on

Figure 6.5 Charlotte demonstrates how to navigate through the program to two children from the mainstream programme.

Tuesday TTT'. He selects the sight word for Tuesday and then loses interest when the discussion continues with 'Weather is cold. Tomorrow is Wednesday.' Sally selects Wednesday and is invited to attach this word to the board. The word falls off and Brendan attempts to fix up the attachment of the word to the board after Sally was unsuccessful. He successfully completes the task. He returns to the mat but then turns away and moves around on the mat while the rest of the group continue their discussion. The children were then directed to desks to complete a worksheet that focused on people in the community and postal services. The worksheet involved reading several familiar words, cutting and pasting. This task appeared to have little interest or connection for Brendan.

During the discussion of the observations of literacy learning at school at the following research meeting, Chris indicated that literacy learning at school seemed to be focused on text-based literacy experiences. She noted that signing and repetition were key elements of the approaches used and that there was little evidence of the integration of Brendan's skills on the computer within literacy learning. When asked about the school literacy programme,

Brendan's teacher commented that literacy learning at school happens during more formal learning time and computer use is more associated with free play. This was also evident in the following observations undertaken by the researcher during a school visit:

> Brendan has the option to work on the computer during a free play period. Chris (his preschool teacher from last year) joins him at the computer and he responds positively to this. Brendan has a brief sign-ing conversation with Chris and opens a Winnie-the-Pooh program on the computer. His responses to the visual cues are very quick and he has strong skills when manipulating the mouse. Brendan appears much more highly engaged than in the formal literacy time. He watches closely and traces the colour pink. Chris supports Brendan's participation by verbally scaffolding and pointing – 'Maybe come back here. You did it.' Brendan responds positively to the instant feedback offered by the program as evidence of success. He claps his hands and looks at Chris. Chris gives physical and auditory responses by offering a 'high five' with her hand and enthusiastically calling out 'High five'. She continues adding her own verbalizations that reinforce the sound of the computer. Brendan responds enthusiastic-ally to the rhythm of the sounds in the program by moving his body in time. He has a quick response to the next cue, says 'J' – 'jai' – and shows a joyful response to the shared experience with Chris. Chris affirms this expression of an emotional response as well as comment-ing that Brendan knows the patterns and sequences within the pro-gram. Brendan manages some word matching independently and for 'mop' says mop, and then says 'm'. Chris reinforces the rhythm and action within the program with her own physical and gestural responses. Brendan shows obvious pleasure at his success, saying 'too good' 'j'. The children then have a break for morning tea. After morn-ing tea Brendan returns to computer joined by two other children, V and Rachel who stand near the computer. Brendan pulls Rachel's hand towards the mouse, he then stands and allows Rachel to sit on the chair.

In this observation, the combination of visual, auditory and gestural feedback offered by the computer and supported by Chris helped to retain Brendan's interest in the literacy experience. Brendan responded well to Chris's scaffolding and her availability in sharing the experience with him. In this context he is able to respond appropriately to quite complex instructions (e.g. 'start with the coloured dot'). In contrast, this level of task commitment, receptive language and comprehension was less evident in the more formal teacher-directed literacy experience. Chris commented that she was pleased to see that Brendan continued to be interested in the social possibilities of the computer at school since this had been an area of difficulty for him while at preschool. She did, however, note that there was only one chair placed at the computer and therefore no physical support for peer interaction and peer scaffolding, and expressed some frustration at the lack of continuity between the preschool and school experience.

These learning scenarios highlight the impact of pedagogical choices for children's learning. The implementation of a strengths-based approach in the preschool facilitated literacy learning as well as social interaction and effective collaboration with peers for children with ASD and language delay and their peers, and this continued to be evident in the computer play shared with Chris at school. The use of ICT and the pedagogy of multiliteracies evident in Chris's interactions assisted Brendan with the complex areas of self-expression, language use, emotional awareness, creativity and problem solving in the learning scenario above. Greater knowledge of Brendan's strengths with the computer, as evident in the preschool environment, could have facilitated his more effective integration at school as well as greater interest in and success with literacy learning. Chris commented that the teaching strategies which had proven so effective in the preschool in supporting Brendan's communication skills, social interactions with peers and adults and engagement within the program could be utilized and strengthened within the school classroom environment. Although a holistic approach to learning was evident within some aspects of the special school, the focus on more formal teaching of literacy seemed to limit possibilities for ICT use and the multimodal learning that appeared to work so well for these children. Although Brendan's competence with the computer was noted, the comments of the teacher suggested that this did not seem to be viewed as part of literacy competence but rather as a part of his ability to engage in playful entertainment. It was therefore not explored to the degree that would have enabled Brendan to demonstrate and use his competency within literacy learning, the expertise with ICT and various multimodal forms which he had developed both at home and at the preschool prior to coming to school.

The focus on text-based literacy outcomes is an external pressure on teachers which can mean less time and attention for a broader perspective on literacy as social practice and for collaborative relationships so important for children with ASD. Charlotte and Brendan were able to develop skills of social interaction, collaboration and cooperation via the use of ICT and within a context of a pedagogy of multiliteracies in their preschool experience which might have been extended and utilized effectively within the school context. The results of this investigation offer valuable insights for teachers working with children with diverse abilities in both preschool and school contexts.

Family involvement

The involvement of families in literacy learning is particularly significant for the families of children with disabilities. Research (Light and Kelford Smith 1993; Light *et al.* 1994; Marvin 1994) indicates that children with disabilities receive fewer opportunities for literacy learning in both home and school contexts and that parents tend to have lower expectations and consider literacy development to be a lower priority for their children (Hardman *et al.* 1996; Lian and Alola 1994). For example, Weikle and Hadadian (2004: 659) stated:

> Parents may not feel competent, may lack knowledge on providing literacy experience and may rely too heavily on intervention programs or pre-schools to work on literacy skills. Concerns over inadequate training, lack of time and learning resources are some of the perceptions of parents in trying to help their children learn.

However, when informed about the ways in which multiliteracies work and the value of ICT for literacy learning, parents of the children were able to work with the diverse literacy practices available in their homes and communities and to see themselves as valued participants in their child's literacy learning. Teachers and parents gave voice to their questions and shared their observations with comments such as 'I have been wondering about . . .', 'Have you ever noticed?' This more frequent and reciprocal exchange built stronger relationships with families who frequently have to deal with the complexities of their child's difficult behaviors and learning needs in isolation.

A culture of connection

The change in the dynamics of the pedagogies implemented in these contexts led to changes in the traditional relationships between the children, teachers and families. The reciprocity observed is reflective of aspects of the pedagogy evident within the Reggio Emilia early childhood experience (e.g. Rinaldi 2006). Giamminuti (2006), recalling her experience in the infant and toddler centres of Reggio Emilia, described the process of visible listening and the intensity of the process that came with the many possible ambiguities and interpretations when the encounter went beyond the verbal. It became evident that communication was possible in many forms that were both simple and complex, subtle and full of multiple interpretations:

> The place of encounter is not the truth but the doubt . . . how they relate, how they learn, not what they know but the how. It is about

bending down low and listening with all senses – reflecting most deeply in a relationship of listening – eyes, heart, and touch.

Although Giamminuti is describing her work with infants and toddlers, rather than with children with ASD and language delay, her words found accord with the teachers in our project as they proceeded in their multiliteracies journey with children who had special needs and rights. When working with the children with ASD their teachers described how they needed to learn to look, to listen and to begin to make sense of the complex multimodal nature of communication and self-expression. In this way these children 'offered knowledges from the margins from the under-thought of perspectives, life experiences, hidden histories and the disqualified voices from which to reconceptualise discourses, individual values and actions' (Cannella and Viruru 2004: 123).

The teachers in the project began to find new ways of 'reading' the experiences of the non-verbal children in their class. This included valuing a glance of shared wondering, and seeing the 'rich normality' (Rinaldi 2006) or the extraordinary moments within the children's daily participation in shared play and learning. Documentation and discussion of these very affirming moments had added value for children and families whose lifeworlds were frequently seen as outside mainstream experiences of family life where diverse abilities are constructed as disability and viewed as deficit and disadvantage.

One of the most powerful qualities to emerge from our observations was the sense of community that was so firmly grounded in honouring diversity. The teachers shared the delight that they experienced as they observed children, who had previously operated on the margins of various groups, become increasingly valued members of the group. They observed the emergence of mutual respect as roles and responsibilities were more equitably shared both by the children in the mainstream preschool and those in the early intervention programme, and by adults with all children. There was a growing sense of 'we all belong to each other' which created a culture of connections and community.

Summary

Our work showed that the use of ICT and a multiliteracies perspective supported the teacher's existing commitment to diversity and difference and a 'strengths-based' approach. They were able to draw on children's different abilities and different sociocultural experiences in new ways. They also found that they could use children's existing skills and knowledge, interests and passions to engage them in learning and in teaching others. When understandings of literacy were expanded to include multimodal texts and viewed from a multiliteracies perspective, the educators found that children came with funds of knowledge that had previously been unknown in the classroom context and that those with diverse abilities had many more pathways to literacy than had previously been recognized. In looking and listening for each child's strengths and interests, the educators were able to identify and build on the children's skills and knowledge as multiliterate learners. Discourses of diversity in early childhood were reflected in pedagogy that transformed the perceptions of children with diverse learning profiles from children who are disabled to differently abled, from having no language to many languages, and from illiterate to multiliterate. The notions of inclusion took on new meaning as diversity, rather than being marginalized, became central to pedagogy.

7 Portraits, pedagogies and pathways

Introduction

The implications of recent work on new literacies and multiliteracies are clear. If educators are to identify how best to encourage children as literacy learners and multiliterate young people, they must attend 'closely to what children and communities actually do with texts, old and new, print and multimodal, traditional and radical' (Luke 2006). Furthermore, we believe that children's literacy identities are more effectively created out of their strengths rather than through a focus on what they do not know. This led us to working with teachers in our project to create a multilayered framework of *portraits, pedagogies* and *pathways* that would assist them to better document and understand how to create effective contexts for learning. This documentation consists, first, of a portrait of a child constructed in conjunction with their family and preschool teachers to identify their existing social and literate practices; second, a multiliteracies pedagogical framework that enabled children's practices to be mapped across multimodalities and dimensions of learning; and third, the creation of pedagogical pathways to more effectively support children in their literacy learning and develop competent literacy identities. By constructing these layers our teachers were better able to:

- reconceptualize literacy as multiliteracies
- view a richer picture of children as 'literate' learners based on a sense of their efficacy
- respond to and extend children as multiliteracy learners via a range of pedagogies that included the appropriate use of ICT and multimodal experiences.

In this chapter, we describe the framework and offer an example of one of the young learners in our project. We tell the story of George and then use the information gathered there to show how it can be incorporated into a multiliteracies framework. This not only documents his literacy learning and the activities that are used to support his learning, but also suggests how his learning can be extended in effective and engaging ways.

The story of George

When George was 5 years of age, he attended preschool and Lydia was his teacher. In the following year, at age 6, George attended primary school and Amelia was his preparatory teacher. English is George's second language since he is of Lebanese background, though Lydia reported that he was fairly fluent in English during his preschool year. In her journal Lydia had already noted that George loved to build and make constructions at preschool.

At preschool, Lydia ran a play-based sessional programme where George had access to many play and learning areas, both indoors and outdoors, including various construction materials and computer programs. During the year Lydia trialled various new technologies in her programme, including using a digital camera, various computer software programs and a dictation machine with the preschool children. She also showed the children how to document their own work, drawing and taking photos, recording anecdotes and uploading information on to the computer.

In primary school, George's preparatory class, like all others in the state, had a 2-hour literacy block from 9.00 a.m. until 11.00 a.m. each day. This was referred to as 'CLaSS' (Children's Literacy Success Strategy), and was divided up into 1 hour of reading and 1 hour of writing. The children rotated through a range of literacy activities whilst the classroom teacher worked with a small group of children with similar literacy abilities. Amelia, his preparatory teacher, described her view of literacy as being related to the fundamentals of reading and writing. In contrast, she viewed multiliteracies as a means of integrating units across the curriculum via different types of activities.

George as a literacy learner

In his preschool year, Lydia described George as a confident leader of other children, particularly in the area of construction. George was known to become slightly upset if his construction plans did not work out and other children did not comply with his plans. Lydia remarked that George would stop and say 'No!' when this happened and would either start his project again or let the other children know what his needs were and direct them with specific instructions. For example, he would say, 'It needs to go here.' Lydia noticed that George seemed to have quite a vision for how his constructions should be built as well as their final structure. She felt that George was visually literate, since he was able to create elaborate constructions and also document them both with pencil and paper and in computer graphics programs (Figure 7.1). The spatial relationships between the different media were consistently similar and reflected his ability to adapt his spatial understandings from three dimensions with the blocks into two dimensions with the drawings. Additionally, George was able to articulate the rationale behind his constructions and give clear instructions to others about the mechanics of the construction.

George's preschool constructions

In his preschool year, George was very keen on building and designing, and his teacher Lydia said that he put a lot of time and effort into his creations. Lydia commented that George also did lots of building at home with boxes, blocks, cards and a range of other materials. His work was very intricate. In one session Lydia reported that George had built a railway out of blocks and it was raised up off the carpet and very detailed. George had spent a long time constructing it when another child knocked it down. George was devastated but responded

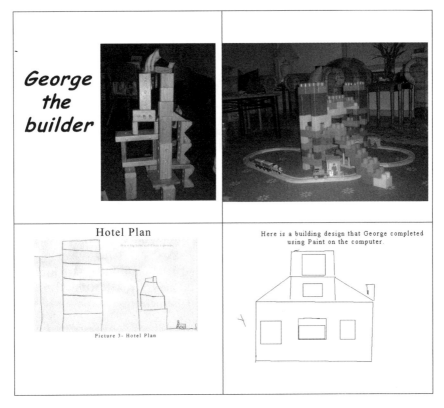

Figure 7.1 George the Builder.

by saying, 'I need to draw it.' He then sat down and drew exactly what he had built, so that he would not forget the structure he had made.

It was a very long process from the original building to drawing it and doing it again. Lydia explained:

> To draw the plan he [George] went and got paper and pastels to draw the plan. The other boys went and followed him. He took the lead and did clouds and the sun. He spent ages working on his plan and the other children were doing their own. He realized that he had a sun and clouds; he didn't have any props for these. He had trees from the train set, but he didn't have the sun and the clouds, so he drew another lot and went and got the masking tape and put it up. The other children were still following his lead, saying, 'Okay George what next?' very excited. When asked what the plan was George replied, 'It is how to fix the railway. We have to do a construction and build it up high.' The he showed his friends how to do it. It was about 30 minutes from when he said he needed to draw it and when he did his plan to how it was originally. His vision was quite concrete.
>
> (Lydia, journal entry)

Lydia was surprised by George's quick thinking when his train construction was knocked over and was taken aback when he said, 'I know how to fix it. I need some paper to draw my design of the train set.' Lydia's image of George, her 'portrait', now included 'quick thinking'. She commented:

> His working from a plan, his vision and his ideas made me realise that he has a lot more going on [inside]. He blows my mind. It was a surprise, just the idea of a plan.
>
> (Journal entry)

Lydia discovered that George took on a leadership role through the process of watching him playing with other children. She also noticed his capacity to visualize as he clearly had a vision of the end product with his block constructions. He knew exactly how he wanted things to be, and other children wanted to play with him. This led to further relational understandings for Lydia, who noted that although George could get frustrated with others, he demonstrated social and relational insight, commenting one day that 'you need to talk to them and sort it out.'

Lydia discovered that George's creations were being supported at home, his mother noting that 'George will find anything and create.' Also at home he was encouraged to keep a book (journal) with all his plans and drawings in it. His mother reported that he would plan things and construct them from there. In another kindergarten session Lydia reported that she and her children were watching the [moon] eclipse live on a website. Lydia explained:

> When we had the eclipse, we were looking at it on the website and the kids were really interested. George went home and made this space book with a pen and he drew pictures of the moon and the sun. He asked his Mum to get things [images] off the internet and the planets. It is this intricate work . . . his mind is just going all the time. Thinking about what he can do . . . At home he has all the equipment available such as masking tape etc., his Mum has provided him.
>
> (Journal entry).

This indicates, among other things, how the teacher's knowledge of George's play experiences and environment at home assisted her in forming her 'portrait' of him as a learner. Lydia's quote also highlights how a portrait of George as a literacy learner in preschool began to emerge as someone who strongly preferred making sense of the world and of himself in that world through spatial and visual modes of communication. This led us to wonder how he would learn in a school environment where the linguistic mode and alphabetic print literacies were privileged. What would happen to a child like George, so clearly confident in his identity as a learner, engaging in sophisticated practices of meaning making and developing his own sense of the world and symbolic representations of this through his constructions? Traditionally, block play and construction are not seen as pathways to print or alphabetic literacy and are frequently only available to children in the preschool years, not in the primary school, where they are expected to make more 'abstract' connections.

Our collective learning as a result of the opportunity to observe and try to understand George was, firstly, the importance of continuing to enable his preferred visual/spatial learning pathway as Lydia had so ably done. Secondly, we questioned how best to harness George's preference for a visual/spatial way of making sense of the world and his experiences. How could this be linked to the learning of alphabetic or print literacy and other modes of communication? The challenge, as we collectively saw it, was how learning in the school context could build on his natural learning inclinations rather than create a sudden 'disconnect' through the exclusive privileging of alphabetic or print literacy.

George's school experience

Amelia, George's first teacher at school, described him as:

> Affectionate, pays attention to detail, always takes pride in his work and is quite confident. He is good on computers and other children rely on him as the expert. He also works well in a group.

When Amelia joined our research project, she brought in some of George's writing samples in response to our request to bring some samples of his work. Amelia's observations of George noted that he had his initial sounds and was beginning to sound out and read words. Her view of George included:

> When he says the word he can put it into his writing. Occasionally he will reverse the 'm' and 'w' letters which is common, he can leave spaces. I just love his drawings as there is so much detail. He is quite a mature drawer and he is beginning to write well. George is left handed and he is Arabic, so at the beginning he went [wrote] from right to left and had back-to-front writing. He is fine now.

Amelia also commented that George was encouraged to play and learn at home, and added an example to his portrait of his mother providing him with an old cheque book from the bank to play with as part of his home office. Amelia had identified and was most supportive of the encouragement of George's mother and his imaginative play.

In his preschool year, George had more freedom to plan, build and construct using a variety of materials, than within his first year of school. For example, Amelia explained that within her literacy classes she used a four-stage plan for the writing activities:

(i)   She talked to children about what they were going to draw.
(ii)   The children drew their picture.
(iii)   The children wrote.
(iv)   A 'conference' occurred between teacher and child, focusing on their individual writing.

Thus, the stimulus for writing was limited to linguistic and visual modes of communication. The challenge for our research was to expand understandings of how children develop their ideas and communication through multiple modes. In Amelia's class, children were provided with some free play/choice times (e.g. when it rained at lunchtime and the children played indoors) and she had noticed that that George would often choose to construct things.

The exchange of stories between Lydia and Amelia and combining the documentation to construct George's portrait enabled a rich multidimensional view of George to be created and shared. The initial portrait of George constructed at primary school valued his visual/linguistic modalities but had not identified his sophisticated visual/spatial modality. Our research created an opportunity for George's preschool and primary teacher to work together, with his family continuing to provide important other evidence about George's social and literate practices. When this broader view of George was shared, a more accurate and richer multiliterate profile and implications for teaching and supporting his literacy development was co-constructed by his teachers.

Over time, the portrait of George captured evidence in different forms. On the wall was a large sheet of paper where his body had been traced. Photos had been stuck to this and provided a talking point about his interests. Amelia also created what we describe as a 'digital suitcase' to enable other forms of evidence to be added to George's portrait. This enabled some of his multimedia work and photostories to be included in his portrait along with recordings of his oral commentary. Her reflections as his teacher were also able to be added, as in consultation with Lydia (who visited George several times during his year with Amelia) she made more multidimensional observations about how George chose to represent his ideas and make meaning. A third form of portrait used by teachers was a special scrapbook. This included drawings and photos by children, learning stories and reflections written by teachers, with comments and additional information provided by parents. These grew over the year and were highly valued by parents and children as a way of perusing and documenting the year. They also provided valuable insight for the child's next teacher, when they moved into Year 1. Another simple but really effective idea, used by Sally, one of the teachers we worked with, was to send each child home with a lunch-sized paper bag and a note to invite the child's family to help them to select items to fill the bag with 'useful junk' – broken jewellery, small plastic containers and lids, wool, ribbon, nuts and bolts, lids, corks, shells, unwanted bric-a-brac and the like. Once all the bags were returned with something inside, the children were invited to share their bags in circle time with the rest of the class. It was a great opportunity for children to talk about their home, family and life experiences and, for some children, having an experience to connect to a familiar object afforded them an opportunity to recount events and it gave the Sally an opportunity to add to her portrait of each child. In this case, their oral language and ability to recount and classify were readily documented through photographs, audio recordings and anecdotes. For example, Alka explained, 'this button is from the yellow jumper my granny knitted for me when I was a baby', this led to a conversation about Alka's family, her favourite colours and her recent holiday. With a collection of seemingly unrelated objects came a recognition by the group that artefacts have meaning and that people have 'special' things and memories all around them. The children devised criteria for sorting the materials they had collected into groups for use in games, collage, construction, mathematics and language groups. They had begun to see objects as a means of communicating stories and events in multiple modes.

Portraits

The multiliteracies portrait is a construction (and documentation) of the interests, capabilities and preferences of a child based on what they can and are inclined to do. It also captures children's home and community social and literate practices, which we have indicated throughout this book are important for learning. The portrait provides a starting point for teachers to work out how to make connections between school and home practices so that children are better able to link their learning and realize that their existing skills and knowledge are valued at school.

The multiliteracies portrait constructs an 'image' of the child as competent and capable in their world. By extending the kinds of evidence that is collected and valued, teachers are able to communicate a broader set of values in relation to literate practices and thus continue supporting the development of a child's literacy identity. At the same time they are able to help and identify a family's view of what is valued as literate practice in contemporary times.

Working with the teachers in this project helped us to identify some of the important features that need to be discussed in conversations with families as well as prompts that could be sent home to help construct the portrait. The first related to the child's interests and their natural inclinations. What sorts of things did they show interest in at home, with their extended family and in their community? When did they seem most engaged, interested and curious? Families were encouraged to take or select photos that represented these particular interests of their child, with a small disposable or digital camera taken home for a weekend to assist with this. Photos could be of people, activities, objects or games. Thus families, who knew the most about the child, were recruited to assist in creating a visual and linguistic portrait of their child. Children were encouraged to take photos of their world and interests, and quickly picked up how to use the camera. From here the beginnings of a visual portrait could be constructed.

Teachers also created opportunities at school to observe children at play and note their preferences. This was an important time, noting which activities children were drawn to repeatedly, choices they made and how they made use of available resources. In particular, teachers looked for evidence as to how children chose to represent their ideas and make meaning, also taking photographs and making anecdotal notes. The provision of time for preschool teachers and primary school teachers to co-construct a child's portrait, drawing on each other's documentation, proved invaluable. The environment of the preschool had often provided those teachers with the opportunity to view a much wider range of social and multiliterate practices than those that schools had traditionally enabled. George the builder is a case in point.

Constructing the multiliteracies portrait of George

How does a teacher go about constructing a multiliteracies portrait? Initially we started with a group of questions that was co-constructed with research

Portrait development prompts	Example of George
What does the child like and show interest in? 	Building, drawing, making things. 
When and how are they most engaged, interested and curious?	Investigating, creating, making things. Generally engaged, interested and curious
What can the child do and how do they represent their ideas and make meaning?	Intricate drawings and buildings in particular
What choices do they make and how do they choose to communicate and make sense of things?	Builds or makes reconstructions of experiences or ideas
What resources can/do they choose to access?	Blocks, cardboard shapes, boxes, cards, tape, paper, scrap materials
What evidence is there of the child actively designing, inquiring, initiating?	See anecdotes and learning stories
What do they wonder about?	How things in the world work

Figure 7.2 A multiliteracies portrait of George.

teachers. This is outlined in Figure 7.2 with an example drawn from our knowledge of George.

Teachers translated these questions into practical activities that they believed enabled them to construct a useful profile of each child and their learning preferences. Some ideas they recommended were:

- Either send home a disposable camera for the child to use or ask parents to take digital photos of the things their child most likes doing at home or in their community. Also provide children with an opportunity to take photos of three things they most like doing at school.
- Parents and child put together a collection of things they want to share (photos, objects, etc.).

- Provide children with an opportunity where they tell or show you what they like to do or things that are important to them.
- Create a digital suitcase – put things in the suitcase that tell you about the child.
- Develop a portfolio or learning story of each child's learning journey.

Teachers also worked out a range of ways to identify the obvious modes that children demonstrated a preference for:

- What a parent or child says they love.
- Give child an enlarged photo of themselves – things I like to see/ watch, things I like to do, things I like to think about, what I like to talk about, what I like to play, things I like to design or build, things I like to listen to, places I like to be, people I like to be with, things I can do.
- Teachers send home a blank A3 sheet and everyone who sees the child traces their hand and says something they know about the child.

Pedagogies

New learning in early childhood requires a pedagogical approach that encompasses multimodal dimensions of learning. A teacher's pedagogical approach – how they plan for learning in their classrooms and respond reflexively to the strengths and needs of each child – can be guided by our multiliteracies pedagogical framework. Constructing and documenting the framework, with examples of young children's entry level and advanced practices, was a way of organizing what was learned that assisted teachers to plan more effectively and richly for each learner. By compiling examples of children's practices within the multiliteracies pedagogical framework, teachers were able to see more options for learning and subsequently construct creative pathways to print literacy as required by the traditional school curriculum (see Appendix 1 for an example).

Teachers in the research did not see a need for every child in the class to have their practices mapped across the multiliteracies pedagogical framework. For many, just the act of the portrait creation was enough for them to make judgements that enabled effective literacy learning. Where teachers found the pedagogical framework particularly helpful was with children who did not progress as expected with print literacy. The framework enabled them to think more precisely and systematically about what strategies were needed to advance the learning of particular children. The multiliteracies pedagogical framework then provided teachers with a way to better understand the learning needs of the children. The framework also assisted with children like George, where the portrait revealed a strong learning preference that needed to be acknowledged, valued and assessed as part of his literacy learning.

A challenge for our project was to co-construct the multiliteracies pedagogical framework with teachers in a way that brought together researcher knowledge about multiliteracies learning and teacher knowledge about young children's learning. What was significant about the research and the framework was the collaborative process. University academics and teachers worked together to clarify different elements that were valued and complementary. This then led to greater insights and understandings so that the final framework was useful for teachers to use in practice. Therefore, while we are able to provide actual examples of what evidence we might see from children in relation to the dimensions of learning and multimodalities in the framework (Appendix 1), we would encourage teachers to co-construct their own representative examples from what they have seen in their classrooms.

Our multiliteracies pedagogical framework was designed to assist teachers to make decisions about the best entry points for children's literacy learning that enable their identity to grow from their strengths. It also acts to identify the complexities and sophistication of children's literate practices that are not often visible in traditional testing techniques.

The framework has been constructed across four dimensions of learning and four communication modalities that are in addition to the linguistic mode that is more commonly exclusively associated with literacy learning. Each modality was mapped across the relational, foundational, critical and creative dimensions of learning which were discussed in Chapter 3. As teachers observed evidence of a child operating in a particular mode, they simply marked (by shading) the degree to which this evidence has been demonstrated. By cross-referencing in this manner, we ensured that new learning in early childhood is more than simply acknowledging children's multimodality. In the teaching and learning context, teachers plan for and are alert to noticing the emergence of foundation skills and knowledge together with children's relational understandings, insight and connections. They actively foster and encourage children to step back and critically analyse or question the way things are and provide diverse opportunities for children to explore and realize their ideas through creative collaboration and action.

By interrogating the multiliteracies pedagogical framework, teachers in our research made it their own, redefining language so that it was meaningful to them and working out what would constitute entry-level and more advanced literate practices from their observations and knowledge of children. While the example (Appendix 1) provides a detailed elaboration of children's practices in response to each dimension of learning and in each communication mode, this is artificial to some extent, as each mode is singled out for individual attention. In reality, children often demonstrated simultaneous practices across multiple modes – visual/spatial as seen in the example of George, or aural/gestural in the example of Alex (Chapter 4). However, the act of defining children's literate practices in response to each dimension of learning in the multiliteracies pedagogical framework was an important factor enabling teachers to construct their own theory–practice connections or praxis.

The children's practices listed in our framework example illustrate how young children in kindergarten and preschool could be observed demonstrating literate practices across all of the modes of communication and dimensions of learning, with both entry-level and, in some cases, advanced-level practices identified. In the case of George, for example, advanced visual/spatial practices were observed in his preschool years, but this was not the case for other children in the research.

The multiliteracies pedagogical framework and associated examples of children's practices enabled teachers to more accurately assess children's literacy development from a multiliteracies viewpoint. When added to traditional measures of linguistic aptitude, a more rounded picture of a child as a literacy learner was established. Teachers used the framework to identify which modes and at what level children demonstrated, acknowledged these to children and let them know such practices were valued, then designed children's pathway to literacy learning from this position of strength. This pathway incorporated children's journeys into alphabetic literacy.

The multiliteracies pedagogical framework is therefore the result of analysis of the learning opportunities provided by teachers, the level of communication about home, school and community practices and the relationships teachers have with children and their families and their capacity to observe, interpret and analyse information.

Pathways

The construction of a portrait and examples of children's associated practices within the multiliteracies pedagogical framework highlighted the differing pedagogies between preschool and school, and the type of learning that was initially valued in each setting. In the preschool setting, the multiliterate nature of the learning opportunities enabled George's building and construction processes to be revealed. They were encouraged and valued as this type of learning was seen to be a regular part of the programme and therefore aligned with George's direct interests and strengths. In contrast, construction processes, visual and spatial literacy were not focused on to any significant extent in the school classroom due to other pressures and a literacy curriculum that mainly centred on improving the children's reading and writing skills.

After George's primary teacher joined the research project and began her interactions with his preschool teacher and the research team, she introduced learning opportunities into her curriculum that enabled George's visual and spatial literacy to be catered for. Her classroom space did not allow for a large block corner to be set up, but she was able to introduce Lego constructions and also introduced animations as a way of addressing her goals for the children to create narratives. In doing so she provided a pathway in which George's strengths were clearly evident.

Amelia initially brainstormed possible ideas for children's Lego animation work with a group of four children that included George. The children had recently been to the zoo on a school excursion and wanted to make a story about the events of the day. Amelia explained the animation process to the children. They needed to take digital photographs of their Lego creation so that each change was a separate shot that would be used in sequence once the photos had been loaded on the computer. In their group of four they worked together so that each member controlled an animal on the set and they helped each other to take photos of that animal in the various stages of motion. The teacher assisted the children to download the photographs and showed them how to play them in sequence to create the animation effect. George was very proud of his achievements and looked extremely pleased with the result. He explained to his preschool teacher, when she came to visit, that he liked building the set and working on the Lego animation. The Lego animation experience also enabled George and his friends to demonstrate their competence in planning, designing and constructing the animation set and their cooperation and organization in directing their Lego animals for their photo shoot.

By the end of George's first year at school, Amelia noted that she suspended judgement when observing George and took more time to notice what he was doing. This led to her seeing new layers of meaning in what he was doing and how he was making sense of particular activities. This was often different from other children, but no less meaningful. One example she gave was a day where she had assumed that George was off-task and just fiddling with some letter blocks. Instead of jumping in and redirecting him back on task, she observed for a little longer and noticed that he was actually completing the task but in a different way than she had expected. George had incorporated the letter blocks into patterns that resulted in a similar outcome to the written task.

The construction of the multiliteracies portrait and alignment of children's practices within the pedagogical framework enabled George's talent and preference for visual and spatial literacy to be revealed, recognized, valued and built on. His personal motivations to plan and build things were then harnessed to support and further extend his literacy learning.

The multiliteracies pathways

The idea of a multiliteracies pathway developed out of discussions with teachers about how to best harness the collective knowledge that was growing out of the professional collaborations of teachers and researchers. This became a way of structuring an action learning process for teachers.

Continuing with the example of George, our research identified that he would clearly benefit from opportunities to operate in more modalities. The pathways planner was designed to assist teachers to think through how they might best design new learning experiences for a learner, such as George, that would be relevant and meaningful. We also created a series of questions to guide the pedagogical decision making of teachers in response to multimodal literacy learners. They are illustrated below, using George's story as the basis for their creation:

- What would literacy practices look like if the school pedagogy accommodated George's unique visual and spatial literacy abilities, his prior experiences and his contextual knowledge?
- What resources would George choose to use to communicate his knowledge and skills if given more choice?
- If George were more actively involved in designing, inquiring and initiating learning, what would the pedagogy look like?

A planner (Appendix 2) was collaboratively generated, trialled and fine-tuned by teachers as a way of scaffolding teacher planning for a child whom they were finding particularly challenging and to enable a focused approach for decision making about the pedagogies and practices that might be used to engage them in new learning. This pedagogical approach is consistent with calls for more 'personalized learning' (Department for Education and Skills 2005) and the need to tailor teaching to children's learning abilities.

Summary

In this chapter we have provided a detailed account of a multiliteracies peda-gogical framework for teaching, learning and assessing multiliterate outcomes that developed during the project. In addition, a multiliteracies portrait that articulated a child's strengths and communication preferences was illustrated as well as describing how the multiliteracies pedagogical framework could be used to construct learning pathways that provided children with personalized learning approaches that built on strengths initially and later expanded to a full repertoire of communication modalities.

We described how we grounded the creation of these frameworks in the knowledge and understandings of teachers and the reciprocal ways in which the construction of the framework enabled teachers to work with children in more enabling ways.

This chapter builds on the notion of 'reimaging' the child through the idea of portraits that encouraged teachers to identify children's learning preferences through a range of informal play activities and observations from within and beyond the education setting.

A consideration of a multiliteracies pedagogical framework and subsequent learning pathways was regarded as a practical way to plan for responsive learning opportunities for children, with explicit examples provided to illustrate a continuum of learning.

8   Pathways to the future

Stop thinking in terms of limitations and start thinking in terms of possibilities.
(Terry Josephson)

Introduction

This final chapter is a synthesis of the main ideas that have been generated throughout this book. We review the implications of conducting research in early childhood centres and schools with teachers as partners. The ideas are drawn together and their impact on the lives of young children in the twenty-first century is explicated and discussed.

Rethinking learning

In this book we have suggested that rethinking learning requires a much broader conceptualization of learning that goes beyond traditional parameters that are measured in quantifiable and observable components in the early childhood years. We have used the example of becoming multiliterate to illustrate the ways in which young children are capable of understanding, making sense of and communicating concepts and ideas in multimodal ways, and how they can frequently incorporate the effective use of ICT to strengthen and amplify their learning. For teachers, adopting this broader perspective requires that they recognize and consider learner subjectivities, diversity and engagement with ideas in multimodal forms. These notions resonate with the work of Kalantzis *et al.* (2005: 38–51) who suggested that two conditions need to be met in order for effective learning to take place:

- *Belonging* – by engaging with the learner's identity so that they are engaged with ideas and processes and want to participate in using them.

- *Transformation* – in which the learner goes on a journey from their existing lifeworld, or knowledge base, to a new 'place' that is beyond the original in scope and dimension. This is achieved through scaffolding by teachers and/or peers and by engagement with new ideas and processes.

In this book we have addressed how this can be achieved by presenting particular cases that highlight the issues connected with multiliteracies, multimodality, diversity and identities in Chapters 3, 4, 5 and 6 respectively. We have described and illustrated the ways in which our collaborative work with teachers of young children from age 4, and in the early years of school, generated the creation of a new multiliteracies framework that enabled them to plan for new learning. This facilitated the design of learning contexts that enabled children to demonstrate their capabilities and understandings in a variety of modes of representation and communication forms.

Insights and provocations

This work could not have been carried out with traditional research paradigms. In Chapter 2, we described the project that formed the basis of the empirical data for the book and foregrounded our collaborative work with teachers as co-researchers.

Collaborative reflexive work

Participation in the research project provided the teachers with time to stand back from their work, reflect on their practices and engage in discussion with other teachers. They were encouraged to observe, document and discuss the learning pathways of the children with whom they were working. This enabled them to reflect more deeply on the significance of their daily interactions and involvement with children, colleagues and families. By critically engaging with the complexities and contradictions that emerged, they were able to undertake the collaborative reflexive work of identifying their subjectivities and challenging their existing practices. This was particularly evident in their use of the transformative qualities of diversity and difference in their pedagogy. As in the work of Paley (1984, 1986, 1989, 1990), the foregrounding of diversity and difference provided rich potential for critical analysis. Rather than being marginalized or displaced, diversity in its many forms became central to the reflexive work of children, families and educators. Aspects of difference can become the opportunity for deeper observation, reflection and analysis, for asking questions of why? and how?

From one mode to many

A consideration of the pedagogy of multiliteracies and the use of ICT helped teachers to identify and value the multimodal forms of communication that were used by children with diverse learning experiences and profiles. The recognition that people negotiate and create social relationships with and without language (e.g. Viruru 2001: 35) shifted the focus from solely verbal communication to include visual, kinaesthetic and gestural communications and thus from one mode to many. With greater emphasis on looking and listening for diverse forms of communication, the teachers and children became more aware of the many ways that learning, interaction and communication can take place and as a result how understandings and relationships can be enriched and extended.

Relationships

The constant interplay between the roles of teacher and learner, educator and protagonist, also contributed to building a sense of community where each felt that they had a valued place. This was manifested as the overt valuing and awareness of the contributions made by each participant in the learning environment. It recognizes that external factors are important for accountability in education and sought new ways to address these issues around attainment via alternative pathways that celebrated diversity and creative contributions. Teachers noted that their participation in the research affirmed that learning is relational, made up of a network of experiences, reflective of intersecting subjectivities and embedded in transactions between a range of individuals. The teachers described their desire to maximize opportunities for making connections, with the ideas that they discussed and through the relationships that they built with the children and their families. They found that what emerged through the shared experiences (such as play in its many forms, small-group discussions and singing, moving and signing) were understandings, both mutual and negotiated in nature, that helped to create both individual and collective identities in the community. People belong to communities by virtue of what they have in common, and communication is one way in which they come to possess things in common. Thus, casting a 'broad net' that included the visual, the aural, the kinesthetic, the facial expression, and the gestural, allowed more opportunities for points of connection. As Giamminuti (2006) recognized, 'when we listened with all our senses we were able to create a culture of belonging.'

Foregrounding families

One of the major outcomes from the project documented in this book was that it encouraged teachers to work from a capabilities perspective rather than a deficit model. When working with preschool teachers, this included a recognition of the 'funds of knowledge' (Moll *et al.* 1992) that children bring to formal learning settings from their homes and communities. Additionally, in this work around multiliteracies we were able to share strategies for encouraging learning and literacy in the preschool years with parents. Although the preschool teachers had previously identified the importance of family awareness and involvement, it was evident that their relationships with families were deepened when children's lived experience and diverse family perspectives moved away from the margins and became part of their pedagogical repertoire. In their exploration of play and literacy in young children's worlds, Beecher and Arthur (2001) identify the importance of family perspectives in educational decision making and literacy learning.

In this project family members indicated to the teachers that they felt more confident about engaging with their children around literacy learning and were able to view themselves as participants in the process. Indeed, many indicated that they were not aware that some of the things that they did on a regular basis with their children were literacy!

Participation in the research provided teachers with opportunities to reflect on their practice in professional learning scenarios and enabled them to create contexts for more authentic interactions and reciprocal relationships with families. The teachers in this project genuinely wanted to know and learn about the perspectives of parents and caregivers since doing so enabled them to more clearly understand and act on what they were seeing in their classrooms as they implemented a pedagogy of multiliteracies with ICT in children's learning. When the teachers were able to share documentation of the children's learning, the parents of children were impressed by the creativity and complexity of their children's explorations and investigations. The families who participated in the project became interested in the new understandings of literacy and the various uses of ICT that were introduced, and explored their potential with their children. For example, parents of children frequently identified as 'disadvantaged' were able to see themselves as participants in their child's literacy learning and build on the literacy experiences within their homes and communities. Furthermore, the parents of children with diverse learning profiles were able to begin to see their child's learning strengths as well as their needs. This helped parents to balance their feelings of anxiety and concern for school success, with knowledge about their children as capable learners.

The place of uncertainty

Our observations also revealed that participation in the research disrupted the teachers entrenched, familiar and habituated practices, thus providing a context for them to challenge their existing ideas and practices. Lenz Taguchi (2006: 259) describes this as an ethic of resistance and noted:

> An ethic of resistance refers to a conscious act of thinking deeply about assumptions and taken for granted notions we take with us often without awareness as we engage in our daily work with children. We deconstruct and take apart what we 'know to be true' to reflect on it, to analyse it, criticize it and resist its seductive powers arising from its familiarity.

The boundaries of the teachers' imagination were expanded through their adoption of the role of researcher, and this enabled them to see new possibilities in their work with children and families. Participation in the research project offered teachers new ideas and provided them with additional time, outside their daily work, that entailed collaborative reflection and supported them to pause, consider, notice and reflect on their pedagogies. In discussing this with the teachers, they commented that the pedagogy of multiliteracies offered them a new lens through which they could reflect on and explore their work. They viewed this as an opportunity to think and see their work differently. The uncertainty that came with new ways of doing professional work meant that there was a need to seek out, think about and discuss with colleagues what had not been seen before. It also caused them to actively think of ways to include visual, tactile, auditory, and gestural expressions in their teaching repertoire. It encouraged them to view their children within a context of a multiliteracies portrait and ask (in relation to a particular child) 'What does this mean for you?' in terms of becoming literate. The pedagogy of multiliteracies offered the teachers new ways of *seeing* – new possibilities and motivation for extending their pedagogical repertoire. Their views reflected an openness to the potential of a contextual and flexible curriculum which was a contrast to the limitations they identified when curriculum was imposed and seemed fragmented and linear.

The reflective discussions of the teachers often had a positive flow-on effect to the other members of their teaching teams. For example, explorations with multiliteracies and ICT were taken up by other teachers within their various settings. The teachers were frequently surprised by the ease and fluency of the childrens' use of new technologies and how they demonstrated their knowledge and skill with computers, video cameras, mobile phones, microwave ovens and digital cameras. Deanne (teacher of the toddler group) described some of the multimodal experiences that she introduced to the toddlers in her group:

> The toddlers have been really interested in a Doctor Seuss computer program which was given by some parents. They've been engrossed and they're starting to follow the words and identify things. They say 'finished!' and 'next one' with the prompts. We have thought about what can we take from the children's interest in these stories on the computer to 'told' stories with a book. Now we read the book but stop and the children create sound effects.
>
> We took the microwave into the room for making play dough. The children knew to press the button and wait for a while and when to open the door. They also showed us that they know how to put in a video. They know what to do and the order of events.

The exploration through the lens of multiliteracies allowed even the youngest children to demonstrate their perceptual, physical and language skills and funds of knowledge while engaged in familiar and meaningful tasks.

Transitions

One of the most important aspects that arose out of the project was the need to facilitate effective transitions from preschool to school. This project brought together early childhood educators from diverse settings and enabled conversations about professional practices and pedagogies that were an integral part of their daily lives. This had many benefits, which broadly speaking were related to two issues: pedagogies and the capabilities and capacity of individual children.

The conversations about pedagogies centred around the ways in which a multiliteracies perspective could enhance the experiences and learning for the young children in the various settings. The preschool teachers were relaxed about trying new teaching approaches and felt that they extended the potential of their children to generate new understandings and also represent their ideas in a variety of modalities. The teachers from the early years of school were initially reluctant to deviate from their plans, which were primarily focused on the attainment of print literacy. Much of the anxiety associated with this was connected to high-stakes testing at both the state and national level and was even impacted by international tests that are not conducted with this age cohort. However, over time they came to the realization that if they incorporated other modalities (e.g. visual, aural, kinaesthetic, gestural, spatial) as a point of entry into becoming literate many children were provided with opportunities that they were previously excluded from. The multiliteracies approach also enriched the capabilities of those children who were attuned to print literacy in new and dynamic ways.

Furthermore, when conversations took place between the teachers, it became apparent that they realized the importance of viewing the children's capabilities over a range of tasks in different modalities. The data from this project revealed that when teachers in the early years of school were experiencing what they perceived to be reluctance on the part of some learners, they gained new insights into these children as they talked to their previous teachers. As a consequence, they started to rethink what it means to be a learner in a contemporary classroom and how they could use this information effectively to promote learning in their early years setting. They found that incorporating a pedagogy of multiliteracies into their work enabled them to reach and extend existing literacy (and numeracy) practices as well as open up a whole range of literacy opportunities for some children who had previously been unable to negotiate pathways to becoming literate.

In this way, participating in the research circles not only changed the practice of all the early childhood educators, but also immediately influenced how some of the teachers viewed the learners in their classrooms. The new perspectives gained from this enabled them to take prompt action to assist their children to become literate, both from the conventional perspective as well as in terms of a much wider and contemporary view of becoming multiliterate.

Appendix 1
Multiliteracies pedagogical framework

Dimensions of literacy	Visual mode – drawings, paintings, photos, graphics, video	
Foundational Direct teaching of skills and knowledge, i.e. what visuals mean and how you might use them	**Entry** Responds to visual cues such as photos or graphics to direct to routines, e.g. washing hands, snack time, a sequence of activities Successfully completes repetitive tasks such as jigsaw puzzles Recognizes and responds to road signs	**Advanced** Able to make sense of and interpret the visual world symbolically with diagrammatic representation Able to use symbols to communicate abstract concepts such as speed or other movements
Meaning making Makes connections and uses visual cues for their own purposes	**Entry** Able to make choices from visual cues to decide what to do Creates a link between visual cues and a sequence of actions Able to make a connection between colours and feelings Sequences a series of visual cues to tell a story	**Advanced** Able to interpret feelings and emotions from photos and drawings Can respond to such questions as 'how does the photo make you feel?' Able to construct a mind map with multiple connections Can use colours to communicate a mood

Dimensions of literacy	Visual mode – drawings, paintings, photos, graphics, video	
Critical Analyses contextual cues and relationships to weigh up possible meanings and courses of actions	**Entry** Distinguishes between alternative choices for a particular situation and able to decide and appropriate course of action Uses contextual knowledge to assist evaluation and decision making	**Advanced** Able to analyse why visual advertising shapes people's behaviour Can 'read' possible intentions of those communicating through visual representations
Creative Uses visuals to construct their own meaning and translate ideas	**Entry** Able to construct a photo story using props. Creates a 2D design and uses in 3D construction, e.g. for block and sandpit play	**Advanced** Uses an intricate visual design to map out an idea or experience Translates intentions into a design
Dimensions of Literacy	Spatial mode – construction, design	
Foundational Developing a sense of own space and interpersonal space. A repertoire of skills and knowledge for objects into space	**Entry** Realization of 'fit' in space • Bodies – personal and community space • Objects in space, e.g. jigsaws • Activities in space Can discriminate different shapes such as 'straight' bits to assist in completing puzzles	**Advanced** Understands terms such as length, perimeter and area Knows spatial symbols and can construct a story map Uses symbols and space to represent 3D constructions

	Entry	Advanced
Meaning making Sees links and connections between different spatial representations and constructions	Cause and effect – understands why/how space is taken up Realizes components of objects/bodies in space Sees connections between representations of constructions	**Advanced** Able to follow meaning of maps Can see links between a 2D design and 3D construction Records details of own constructions in a 2D drawing
Critical	Uses strategic thinking to work out a puzzle Works out an order to progress in a puzzle Uses guess and check Goes beyond trial and error	**Advanced** Engages in problem solving when boundaries and limits are given e.g. create a structure with newspaper and tape that is 1 metre tall that the group could sit inside
Creative Designing, developing, making, acting on and realizing ideas	Builds detailed constructions that include order, pattern and form	**Advanced** Builds intricate constructions and can talk to detail Creates a design from an idea and makes a 3D construction

Dimensions of literacy	Aural mode – music, voice tones, sound effects	
Foundational Knowledge of vocabulary to describe sounds and music	**Entry** Identifying sounds and rhythms Following sound patterns Recognizing voice tones	**Advanced** Reads with expression Modulates voice to mood of story
Meaning making Using prior knowledge and life experience to make sense of different sounds, tones and music	**Entry** Demonstrates understanding of the meaning of different voice tones Knows when to use loud and soft voices Recognizes meaning of different sound cues, e.g. bells Can put a sound to a visual, e.g. car skidding	**Advanced** Changes tone and speed of voice to add a layer of meaning Interprets mood from music Communicates via music
Critical Engages in feedback, analysis and comparison	**Entry** Discriminates between different types of music and can comment on cause and effect Can comment on how sounds convey meaning	**Advanced** Able to discuss musical interpretations and responses Able to identify music preferences and explain why Reflects on what works in a musical composition or soundscape
Creative Takes a risk and steps into the unknown to compose	**Entry** Experiments with voice tones and modulations Creates a sound to communicate a mood, object or person	**Advanced** Creates a soundscape as background to a story which includes a sequence of changes. Recognizable beginning, middle and end

Dimensions of literacy	Gestural – body language, facial expressions, social connection		
Foundational Developing a repertoire of gestural communication forms	**Entry** Follows gestural indicators, e.g. pointing, mimicking, facial expressions Uses gestures to make social contact and interact Uses eye contact signals Successfully engages in games requiring gestures to indicate turn takings		**Advanced** Knows, understands and uses the basics of body language and gestural communications Has developed a vocabulary in relation to gestural communication
Meaning making communicating through and interpreting gestural communication forms	**Entry** Can 'read' the meaning behind gestures Able to role play various emotions and communicates needs via gestures. 'Reads' feelings from an image		**Advanced** Interprets meaning of a dance or mime Reads different levels of intensity related to body language Aware of cultural differences for social norms of gestures
Critical Critiquing, analysis and revising actions on receiving feedback about effectiveness	**Entry** Acts out a scenario e.g. from a playground incident, then revises actions using feedback Works out what is needed to communicate such things as friendship, welcome and acceptance Can make suggestions about another child's body language in order to assist social relationships		**Advanced** Uses contextual knowledge to understand meaning of gestures and expressions in different situations
Creative Designing, developing, making, acting on and realizing ideas	**Entry** Can plan and design a simple sequence of actions that tell a story		**Advanced** Can design (plan, negotiate) and organise a complex sequence that tell a story, e.g. mime, dance

Appendix 2
Planning the multiliteracies pathway

Name of child	
Preferred modes of communication (i.e. visual, aural, gestural, spatial)	
To build on their strengths in these modes I will:	
Interests, knowledge and experience the child brings that could provide a foundation for literacy learning	
Foundational skills that are a priority for development	
Ideas for development that utilize strengths and interests	
How the child responded	
Implications for my practice and approach based on the child's response	
Meaning-making skills that are a priority for development	
Ideas for development that utilize strengths and interests	
How the child responded	
Implications for my practice and approach based on the child's response	
Critical thinking skills that are a priority for development	
Ideas for development that utilize strengths and interests	

Name of child	
How the child responded	
Implications for my practice and approach based on the child's response	
Priorities for fostering the child's creativity and applying multiliteracies learning to pursue their own ideas	
Ideas for development that utilize strengths and interests	
How the child responded	
Implications for my practice and approach based on the child's response	

References

Anderson, G.L. and Heer, K. (1999). The new paradigm wars: Is there room for rigorous practitioner knowledge in schools and universities? *Educational Researcher*, 28(5), 12–21, 40.

Armstrong, A. and Casement, C. (2001). *The Child and the Machine: How Computers Put Our Children's Education at Risk*. Carlton: Scribe.

Arthur, L., Beecher, B., Death, E., Dockett, S. and Farmer, S. (2005). *Programming and Planning in Early Childhood Settings*. Sydney: Harcourt Brace.

Australian Council of Deans of Education (2001). *New Learning: A Charter for Action*. Canberra: ACDE.

Bassey, M. (2001). A solution to the problem of generalisation in educational research: Fuzzy prediction. *Oxford Review of Education*, 27(1), 5–22.

Batchelor, D. and Taylor, H. (2005). Social inclusion – The next step: User friendly strategies to promote social interaction and peer acceptance with children with disabilities. *Australian Journal of Early Childhood*, 30(4), 10–16.

Becker, H.J. (2000). Findings from the teaching learning and computing survey: Is Larry Cuban right? *Education Policy Analysis Archives*, 8(51), 1–33.

Beecher, B. and Arthur, L. (2001). *Play and Literacy in Children's Worlds*. Newtown: Primary English Teachers Association.

Bredecamp, S. and Copple, C. (eds) (1997). *Developmentally Appropriate Practice in Early Childhood Programs*, revised edition. Washington, DC: National Association for the Education of Young Children.

Britt, C. and Sumsion, J. (2002). Within the borderlands: Beginning early childhood teachers in primary schools. Presentation at the Association for Australian Research in Education Conference, Brisbane.

Bruner, J. (1977). *The Process of Education*. Cambridge, MA: Harvard University Press.

Cannella, G.S. (1997). *Deconstructing Early Childhood Education: Social Justice and Revolution*. New York: Peter Lang.

Cannella, G.S. and Viruru, R. (2004). *Childhood and Postcolonization: Power, Education, and Contemporary Practice*. New York: RoutledgeFalmer.

Castignetti, M. and Vecchi, V. (eds) (1997). *Shoe and Metre: The Unheard Voice of Children*. Reggio Emilia, Italy: Reggio Children.

Cherednichenko, B., Davies, A., Kruger, T. and O'Rourke, M. (2001). Collaborative practices: From description to theory. Paper presented at the Australian Association for Research in Education, Fremantle, WA.

Clay, M.M. (1993). *An Observation Survey of Early Literacy Achievement*. Portsmouth, NH: Heinemann Education.

Clements, D.H. (1999). Concrete manipulatives, concrete ideas. *Contemporary Issues in Early Childhood*, 1(1), 45–60.

Comber, B. (1997). The problem of 'background' in researching the student subject. Paper presented at the Association for Australian Research in Education Conference, Brisbane.

Comber, B. and Green, B. (1999). *Information Technology: Literacy and Educational Disadvantage*. Adelaide: Department of Education and Training and Employment.

Compton-Lilly, C. (2006). Identity, childhood culture and literacy learning: A case study. *Journal of Early Childhood Literacy*, 6(1), 57–76.

Conners, B. (1991). Teacher development and the teacher. In P. Hughes (ed.), *Teachers' Professional Lives* (pp. 53–81). Hawthorn, Vic.: Australian Council for Educational Research.

Cope, B. and Kalantzis, M. (eds) (2000). *Multiliteracies: Literacy Learning and the Design of Social Futures*. London: Routledge.

Cordes, C. and Miller, E. (2000). *Fool's Gold: A Critical Look at Computers in Childhood*. College Park, MD: Alliance for Childhood.

Creaser, B. and Dau, E. (eds) (1996). *The Anti-Bias Approach in Early Childhood*. Sydney: Harper Educational.

Cuban, L. (1993). Computers meet classroom: Classroom wins. *Teachers College Record*, 95(2), 185–219.

Cummins, J. (2005). Afterword. In K. Pahl and J. Rowsell (eds), *Literacy and Education: Understanding the New Literacy Studies in the Classroom* (pp. 140–52). London: Paul Chapman Publishing.

Daiute, C. (1992). Multimedia composing: Extending the resources of the kindergarten to writers across the grades. *Language Arts*, 69, 250–60.

Department for Education and Skills (2005). *Higher Standards, Better Schools for All: More Choice for Parents and Pupils*, Cm. 6677. Norwich: Stationery Office.

Department of Education, Science and Training (2002). *Raising the Standards: A Proposal for the Development of an ICT Competency Framework for Teachers*. Canberra: Department of Education, Science and Training.

Derman-Sparkes, L. and the ABC Task Force (1989). *Anti-Bias Curriculum – Tools for Empowering Young Children*. Washington, DC: National Association for the Education of Young Children.

Dewey, J. (1899). *The School and Society*. Chicago: University of Chicago Press.

Dockett, S. and Perry, B. (2007). *Starting School: Perceptions, Experiences and Expectations*. Sydney: University of New South Wales Press.

Early Childhood Australia (2007). *Early Childhood Code of Ethics*. Watson, ACT: Author.

Elkind, D. (1996). Young children and technology: A cautionary note. *Young Children*, September, 22–3.

Ely, M., Anzul, M., Friedman, T., Garner, D. and McCormack Steinmetz, A. (1991). *Doing Qualitative Research: Circles within Circles*. London: Falmer Press.

Erikson, E. (1968). *Identity, Youth and Crisis*. New York: Norton.

Erlandson, D.A., Harris, E.L., Skipper, B.L. and Allen, S.D. (1993). *Doing Naturalistic Inquiry*. Newbury Park, CA: Sage.

Fals Borda, O. (2001). Participatory (action) research in social theory: Origins and challenges. In P. Reason and H. Bradbury (eds), *Handbook of Action Research: Participative Inquiry and Practice* (pp. 27–37). Thousand Oaks, CA: Sage.

Finnegan, R. (2002). *Communicating*. London: Routledge.

Fisher, R. and Williams, M. (eds) (2004). *Unlocking Creativity*. London: David Fulton.

Fleer, M. (ed.) (1995). *DAPcentrism: Challenging Developmentally Appropriate Practice*. Canberra: Australian Early Childhood Association.

Fleer, M. (2001). *An Early Childhood Research Agenda: Voices from the Field*. Canberra: Commonwealth of Australia.

Fleet, A. and Lockwood, V. (2002). Authentic literacy assessment. In L. Makin and C. Jones Díaz (eds), *Literacies in Early Childhood: Changing Views, Challenging Practice* (pp. 135–53). Sydney: MacLennan & Petty.

Fleet, A., Patterson, C. and Roberston, J., (2006). *Insights: Behind Early Childhood Pedagogical Documentation*. Castle Hill, NSW: Pademelon Press.

Freire, P. (1972). *Cultural Action for Freedom*. Harmondsworth: Penguin.

Freire, P. (1973). *Education for Critical Consciousness*. New York: Seabury Press.

Gaventa, J. and Cornwall, A. (2001). Power and knowledge. In P. Reason and H. Bradbury (eds), *Handbook of Action Research: Participative Inquiry and Practice* (pp. 70–80). Thousand Oaks, CA: Sage.

Gee, J.P. (1996). *Social Linguistics and Literacies: Ideology in Discourses*, 2nd edition. London: Falmer.

Gee, J.P. (1999). *An Introduction to Discourse Analysis: Theory and Method*. London: Routledge.

Giamminuti, S. (2006). Stories from Arcobelena Infant–Toddler Centre in Reggio Emilia: Culture, research and participation. Presentation at Wondering Conference, Perth.

Gibson, O. (2005). Young blog their way to a publishing revolution. www.guardian.co.uk/technology/2005/oct/07/media.pressandpublishing (accessed 29 October 2007).

Green, B., Reid, J. and Bigum, C. (1998). Teaching the Nintendo generation? Children, computer culture and popular technologies. In S. Howard (ed.), *Wired-Up: Young People and the Electronic Media* (pp. 19–41). London: UCL Press.

Greishaber, S. and Cannella G.S (eds) (2001) *Embracing Identities in Early Childhood Education: Diversity and Possibilities*. New York: Teachers College Press.

Gudjónsdóttir, H., Cacciattolo, M., Dakich, E., Davies, A., Kelly, C. and Dalmau, M.C. (2007). Transformative pathways: Inclusive pedagogies in teacher education. *Journal of Research on Technology in Education*, 40(2).

Haas Dyson, A. (1997). *Writing Superheroes: Contemporary Childhood Popular Culture and Classroom Literacy*. New York: Teachers College Press.

Haas Dyson, A. (2003). *The Brothers and Sisters Learn to Write: Popular Literacies in Childhood and School Cultures*. New York: Teachers College Press.

Hagood, M.C., (2000). New times, new millennium, new literacies. *Reading Research and Instruction*, 39(4), 311–28.

Hall, S. and Jacques, M. (1989). *New Times: The Changing Face of Politics in the 1990s*. London: Lawrence Wishart.

Hammersley, M. and Atkinson, P. (1995). *Ethnography: Principles in Practice*, 2nd edition. London: Routledge.

Hardman, M., Drew, C. and Egan, M. (1996). *Human Exceptionality: Society, School and Family*, 5th edition. Needham Heights, MA: Allyn &Bacon.

Harvey, D. (1989). *The Condition of Postmodernity: An Enquiry into the Origins of Cultural Change*. Oxford: Basil Blackwell.

Healy, J. (1998). *Failure to Connect: How Computers Affect our Children's Minds – for Better and Worse*. New York: Simon & Schuster.

Healy, J. and Honan, E. (eds) (2004). *Text Next: New Resources for Literacy Learning*. Newtown, NSW: Primary English Teachers Association.

Heron, J. and Reason, P. (2001). The practice of co-operative inquiry: Research 'with' rather than 'on' people. In P. Reason and H. Bradbury (eds), *Handbook of Action Research: Participative Inquiry and Practice* (pp. 179–88). Thousand Oaks, CA: Sage.

Hill, S., Yelland, N. and Thelning, K. (2002). Children of the new millennium: Using information and communication technologies for playing and learning in the information age. ARC linkage project, LP0215770.

Hodge, R. and Kress, G. (1988). *Social Semiotics*. Cambridge: Polity Press.

Hopkins, D. (1987). Teacher research as a basis for staff development. In M.F. Wideen and I. Andrews (eds), *Staff Development for School Improvement: A Focus on the Teacher* (pp. 111–28). Philadelphia: Falmer Press.

Howe, N. and Strauss, W. (2000). *Millennials Rising: The Next Great Generation*. New York: Vintage.

IBM Corporation (2000). KidSmart Early Learning Program. http://www.ibm.com/ ibm/ibmgives/downloads/kidsmart.pdf (accessed 6 June 2000).

James, A. and Prout, A. (eds) (1990). *Constructing and Reconstructing Childhood*. Basingstoke: Falmer Press.

Jeffrey, B. and Craft, A. (2004). Teaching creatively and teaching for creativity: Distinctions and relationships. *Educational Studies*, 30(1), 77–87.

Jewitt, C. (2006). *Technology, Literacy and Learning: A Multimodal Approach*. Abingdon: Routledge.

Jewitt, C. and Kress, G. (eds) (2003). *Multimodal Literacy*. New York: Peter Lang.

Kalantzis, M. and Cope, B. (eds) (2001). *Transformations in Language and Learning: Perspectives on Multiliteracies*. Melbourne: Common Ground Publishing.

Kalantzis, M. and Cope, B. (2008). *New Learning: Elements of a Science of Education*. Cambridge: Cambridge University Press.

Kalantzis, M., Cope, B. and the Learning by Design Project Group (2005). *Learning by Design*. Melbourne: Victorian Schools Innovation Commission.

Katz, L. and Chard, S. (2000). *Engaging Children's Minds: The Project Approach*. Stamford, CT: Ablex.

Kemmis, S. (2001). Exploring the relevance of critical theory for action research: Emancipatory action research in the footsteps of Jürgen Habermas. In P. Reason and H. Bradbury (eds), *Handbook of Action Research* (pp. 91–102). Thousand Oaks, CA: Sage.

Kendrick, M. (2005). Playing house: A sideways glance at literacy and identity in early childhood. *Journal of Early Childhood Literacy*, 5(1), 5–28.

Kessler, S. and Swadener, B.B. (eds) (1992). *Reconceptualizing the Early Childhood Curriculum – Beginning the Dialogue*. New York: Teachers College Press.

Kincheloe, J. (1991). *Teachers as researchers: Qualitative Inquiry as a Path to Empowerment*. London: Falmer Press.

Kincheloe, J.L. and McLaren, P.L. (1994). Rethinking critical theory and qualitative research. In N.K. Denzin and Y.S. Lincoln (eds), *Handbook of Qualitative Research* (pp. 138–57). Thousand Oaks, CA: Sage.

Kress, G. (1997). *Before Writing: Rethinking Paths to Literacy*. London: Routledge.

Kress, G. (2003). *Literacy in the New Media Age*. London: Routledge.

Kress, G. and van Leeuwen, T. (1996). *Reading Images: The Grammar of Visual Design*. London: Routledge.

Kress, G. and van Leeuwen, T. (2001). *Multimodal Discourse: The Modes and Media of Contemporary Communication*. London: Arnold.

Kruger, T., Cherednichenko, B., Hooley, N. and Moore, R. (2001). Longitudinal study of school restructuring 1996–2000. Report, Victoria University of Technology.

Labbo, L. (1996). A semiotic analysis of young children's symbol making in a classroom computer centre. *Reading Research Quarterly*, 31(4), 356–85.

Lankshear, C. and Knobel, M. (2004). *New Literacies: Changing Knowledge and Classroom Learning*. Buckingham: Open University Press.

Lankshear, C. and Snyder, I. (2000). *Teachers and Technoliteracy: Managing Literacy, Technology and Learning in Schools*. St Leonards: Allen & Unwin.

Lave, J and Wenger, E. (1990). *Situated Learning: Legitimate Peripheral Participation*. Cambridge: Cambridge University Press.

Lee, L. (2002). Young gifted girls and boys: perspectives through the lens of gender, *Contemporary Issues in Early Childhood*, 3(3), 383–99.

Lenz Taguchi, H. (2006). Reconceptualizing early childhood education: Challenging taken-for-granted ideas. In J. Einarsdóttir and J.T. Wagner (eds), *Nordic Perspectives in Early Childhood Education*. Greenwich, CT: Information Age Publishing.

Leslie, L. and Jett-Simpson, M. (1997). *Authentic Literacy: An Ecological Approach*. New York: Addison Wesley Longman.

Leu, D. (1996). Sarah's secrets: Social aspects of literacy and learning in a digital information age. *The Reading Teacher*, 50(2), 162–5.

Leu, D. (2000a). Our children's future: Changing the focus of literacy and literacy instruction. *The Reading Teacher*, 53, 424–31.

Leu, D. (2000b). Literacy and technology: Deictic consequences for literacy education in the information age. In M. Kamil, P. Mosenthal, P. Pearson and R. Barr (eds), *Handbook of Reading Research*, Vol. 3 (pp. 745–72). Mahwah NJ: Lawrence Erlbaum Associates.

Leu, D.J., Jr. (2002). The new literacies: Research on reading instruction with the Internet and other digital technologies. In A.E. Farstrup and S.J. Samuels (eds), *What Research Has to Say about Reading Instruction*, 3rd edition (pp. 310–37). Newark, DE: International Reading Association.

Lian, M.J. and Alola, G. (1994). Parental responses, roles and responsibilities in S.K. Alper, P.J. Schloss and C.N. Schloss (eds), *Families and Students with Disabilities* (pp. 51–94). Boston: Allyn & Bacon.

Light, J., Binger, C. and Kelford Smith, A.K. (1994). Story reading interactions between preschoolers who use ACC and their mothers. *Augmentative & Alternate Communication*, 10(4), 258–68.

Light, J. and Kelford Smith, A.K. (1993). The home literacy experiences of preschoolers who use AAC systems and of their non disabled peers. *Augmentative & Alternate Communication*, 9(1), 10–25.

Lincoln, Y. and Guba, E. (1985). *Naturalistic Inquiry*. Beverly Hills, CA: Sage.

Livingstone, S. and Bober, M. (n.d.) UK children go online: Surveying the experience of young people and their parents. LSE Research online. http://eprints.lse.ac.uk (accessed 4 December 2007).

Luke, A. (1994). *The Social Construction of Literacy in the Classroom*. Melbourne: Macmillan.

Luke, A. (2006). Foreword. In K. Pahl and J. Rowsell (eds), *Literacy and Education: Understanding the New Literacy Studies in the Classroom* (pp. x–xiv). London: Paul Chapman Publishing.

Luke, A. and Freebody, P. (1999). Further notes on the four resources model. http://www.readingonline.org/research/lukefreebody.html (accessed 31 March 2008).

Luke, A. and Freebody, P. (2000). *Literate Futures: The Teacher Summary Version*. Brisbane: State of Queensland (Department of Education).

Luria, A.R. (1976). *Cognitive Development: Its Cultural and Social Foundations*. Cambridge, MA: Harvard University Press.

MacNaughton, G. (2000). *Rethinking Gender in Early Childhood Education*. St Leonards: Allen & Unwin.

Maguire, P. (2001). Uneven ground: Feminisms and action research. In P. Reason and H. Bradbury (eds), *Handbook of Action Research: Participative Inquiry and Practice*. Thousand Oaks, CA: Sage.

Makin, L., Jones Díaz, C. and McLachan, C. (2007). *Literacies in Childhood – Changing Views, Challenging Practice*. Marrickville, NSW: Maclennan and Petty.

Malaguzzi, L. (1994). History, ideas and basic philosophy In C. Edwards, L. Gandini and G. Forman (eds), *The Hundred Languages of Children*. Norwood, NJ: Ablex.

Marsh, J. (2004). *BBC Child of Our Time: Young Children's Use of Popular Culture, Media and New Technologies*. Sheffield: University of Sheffield.

Martin, J. R. and Veel, R. (1998). *Reading Science. Critical and Functional Perspectives on Discourses in Science*. New York: Routledge.

Martinec, R. (2000). Types of processes in action. *Semiotica*, 130(3/4), 243–68.

Marvin, C. (1994). Home literacy experience of preschool children with single and multiple disabilities. *Topics in Early Childhood Special Education*, 21(30), 22–42.

McCarthey, S.J. and Moje, E.B. (2002). Identity matters. *Reading Research Quarterly*, 37(2), 228–38.

Mishler, E. G. (1990). Validation in inquiry-guided research: The role of exemplars in narrative studies. *Harvard Educational Review*, 60(4), 415–42.

Moje, E. B., Ciechanowski, K. M., Kramer, K., Ellis, L., Carrillo, R., and Collazo, T. (2004). Working toward third space in content area literacy: An examination of everyday funds of knowledge and discourse, *Reading Research Quarterly* 39(1), 38–70.

Moll, L. C., Amanti, C., Neff, D. and Gonzalez, N. (1992). Funds of knowledge for teaching: Using a qualitative approach to connect homes and classrooms. *Theory into Practice*, 31(2), 132–41.

Monteith, M. (ed.) (2004). *ICT for Curriculum Enhancement*. Bristol: Intellect.

New London Group. (1996). A pedagogy of multiliteracies. *Harvard Educational Review*, 60(1), 66–92.

Noffke, S.E. and Stevenson, R.B. (1995). *Educational Action Research: Becoming Practically Critical*. New York: Teachers College Press.

NSW Office of Child Care (2002). *The NSW Curriculum Framework – The Practice of Relationships*. Sydney: Author.

O'Rourke, M. (2003). Technology and educational change: Making the links. Unpublished dissertation, Victoria University, Melbourne.

O'Rourke, M. (2005). Multiliteracies for 21st century schools. *ANSN Snapshot*, 2, 1–14.

O'Toole, M. (1994). *The Language of Displayed Art*. London: Leicester University Press.

Pahl, K. and Rowsell, J. (2005). *Literacy and Education: Understanding the New Literacy Studies in the Classroom*. London: Paul Chapman.

Pahl, K and Rowsell, J. (eds) (2006). *Travel Notes from the New Literacy Studies: Instances of Practice*. Clevedon: Multilingual Matters.

Paley, V.G. (1984). *Boys and Girls*. Chicago: University of Chicago Press.

Paley, V. G. (1986). *Wally's Stories*. Cambridge, MA: Harvard University Press.

Paley, V.G. (1989). *White Teacher*. Cambridge, MA: Harvard University Press.

Paley, V.G. (1990). *The Boy who Would Be a Helicopter*. Cambridge, MA: Harvard University Press.

Papert, S. (1980). *Mindstorms: Children, Computers, and Powerful Ideas*. Brighton: Harvester.

Papert, S. (1998). *The Connected Family: Bridging the Digital Generation Gap*. Atlanta, GA: Longstreet.

Partnership for 21st Century Skills (n.d.) Learning for the 21st century. www.21stcenturyskills.org (accessed 25 December 2007).

Piaget, J. (1972). *The Principles of Genetic Epistemology*. New York: Basic Books.

Piannfetti, E. (2001). Teachers and technology: Digital literacy through professional development. *Language Arts*, 78(3), 255–62.

Plowman, L. and Stephen, C. (2007). Guided interaction in pre-school settings. *Journal of Computer Assisted Learning*, 23, 14–26.

Rideout, V., Vandewater, E. and Wartella, E. (2003). Zero to six: Electronic media in the lives of infants, toddlers and preschoolers. http://eric.ed.gov:80/ERICWebPortal/custom/portlets/recordDetails/detailmini.jsp?_nfpb=true&_&ERICExtSearch_SearchValue_0=ED482302&ERICExtSearch_SearchType_0=no&accno=ED482302 (accessed 25 December 2007).

Rinaldi, C. (2006). *In Dialogue with Reggio Emilia – Listening, Researching and Learning*. New York: Routledge.

Robinson, K. and Jones Díaz, C. (2006). *Diversity and Difference in Early Childhood: Implications for Theory and Practice*. Buckingham: Oxford University Press.

Rowsell, J. (2006). *Family Literacy Experiences: Creating Reading and Writing Opportunities that Support Classroom Learning*. Markham, Ont.: Stenhouse.

Sarup, M. (1998). *Identity, Culture and the Postmodern World*. Athens: University of Georgia Press.

Sawyer, A. (2000). Preschool teachers in primary schools; stories from the field. *Contemporary Issues in Early Childhood*, 1(3), 339–44.

Scardamalia, M. (2003). Extending the limits of the possible in education. Keynote address, International Conference for Educational Technology, Hong Kong.

Searle, J.R. (1993). The problem of consciousness. *Consciousness and Cognition*, 2, 310–19.

Selener, D. (1997). *Participatory Action Research and Social Change*. Ithaca, NY: Cornell Participatory Action Research Network.

Silin, J.G. (1995). *Sex, Death and the Education of Children: Our Passion for Ignorance in the Age of AIDS*. New York: Teachers College Press.

Stake, R. (1987). An evolutionary view of programming staff development. In M.F. Wideen and I. Andrews (eds) *Staff Development for School Improvement* (pp. 55–69). Philadelphia: Falmer Press.

State of South Australia, Department of Education and Children's Services and University of South Australia (2006). *Mapping Multiliteracies: A Professional Learning Resource*. Adelaide: DECS Publishing.

Stenhouse, L. (1976). *An Introduction to Curriculum Research and Development*. London: Heinemann.

Steering Committee for the Review of Government Service Provision, Commonwealth of Australia (2005). *Overcoming Indigenous Disadvantage: Key Indicators 2005*. Melbourne: Commonwealth of Australia.

Stein, P. (2003). The Olifantsvlei fresh stories project: Multimodality, creativity and fixing in the semiotic chain. In C. Jewitt and G. Kress (eds), *Multimodal Literacy* (pp. 12–138), New York: Peter Lang.

Sumsion, J. (2006). From Whitlam to economic rationalism and beyond: A conceptual framework for political activism in children's services. *Australian Journal of Early Childhood*, 31(1), 1–8.

Tinker, R. (1999). New technology bumps into an old curriculum: Does the traditional course sequence need an overhaul? http://www.concord.org/publications/newsletter/1999winter/newtechnology.html (accessed 4 February 2008).

United States Department of Education (2001). No Child Left Behind. Executive summary. http://www.ed.gov/rschstat/landing.jhtml?src=rt (accessed 4 February 2008).

Van Leeuwen, T. (1999). *Speech, Sound, Music*. Basingstoke: Macmillan.

Vincent, J. (2005). Multimodal literacies in the school curriculum: an urgent matter of equity. In A Méndez-Vilas (ed.), *Recent Research Developments in Learning Technologies*. Badajoz, Spain: Formatex. http://www.formatex.org/micte2005/book.htm (accessed 31 March 2008).

Viruru, R. (2001). Colonized through language: The case of early childhood education. *Contemporary Issues in Early Childhood*, 2(1), 31–47.

Vygotsky, L. (1962). *Thought and Language*. Cambridge, MA: MIT Press.

Vygotsky, L.S. (1978). *Mind in Society: The Development of Higher Psychological Processes*. Cambridge MA: Harvard University Press.

Wagner, J. (1997). The unavoidable intervention of educational research: A framework for reconsidering researcher–practitioner cooperation. *Educational Researcher*, 26(7), 13–22.

Wartella, E. and Jennings, N. (2000). Children and computers: New technology – old concerns. *Children and Computer Technology*, 10(2), 31–43.

Weber, S. (1992). A universidade e a qualidade da educação pública. *Em Aberto*, 11(53), 64–72.

Weikle, B. and Hadadian, A. (2004). Literacy development and disabilities: Are we moving in the right direction? *Early Childhood Development and Care*, 174(7–8), 651–66.

Wolcott, H.F. (1992). Posturing in qualitative inquiry. In M.D. LeCompte, W.L. Millroy and J. Preissle (eds), *The Handbook of Qualitative Research in Education* (pp. 3–52). New York: Academic Press.

Yeatman, A. and Sachs, J. (1995). Making the links: A formative evaluation of the first year of the innovative links between universities and schools for teacher professional development. Perth, WA: Murdoch University.

Yelland, N.J. (1997). Young children's understanding of paths and measurement. *Mathematics Education Research Journal*, 10(1), 83–99.

Yelland, N. (2001). *Teaching and Learning with Information and Communication Technologies (ICT) for Numeracy in the Early Childhood and Primary Years of Schooling.* Canberra: Department of Education, Training and Youth Affairs.

Yelland, N.J. (2002). Creating microworlds for exploring mathematical understandings in the early years of school. *Journal of Educational Computing Research,* 27(1–2), 77–92.

Yelland, N.J. (2007). *Shift to the Future: Rethinking Learning with New Technologies in Education.* London: Taylor & Francis.

Index